The Self-Healing Cookbook

by Kristina Turner

Earthtones Press

<u>Note:</u>

This handbook is designed as an educational
tool for better health. Recipes and
information on traditional home remedies
are included as examples for you to
learn from. They are not diagnostic
or prescriptive.

Everyone's health needs are different.
I encourage you to listen to your own
body, and complement this information
with the advice of qualified health
professionals.

"The Art of Medicine consists
of amusing the patient,
while nature cures the
disease."

                    - Voltaire

1987, 1988, 1994, 1996, 1998, 2000, 2002 by Kristina Turner

Ninth revised edition. All rights reserved.
Cover, text & illustrations by the author.

Library of Congress Catalog Card Number: 88-80506
ISBN 0-945668-15-5

Printed in the United States
30 29 28 27

EARTHTONES PRESS * P.O. Box 411, Vashon Island, WA 98070

TABLE OF CONTENTS

Table of Contents (Cont.)

Take a break from cooking. Use this mini-
workbook to gain a systematic understanding of
how symptoms develop. Prevention Checklists.
What to expect as you change your diet.
Visualization and journal exercises to help
you participate more fully in your own healing.

Turn here when you want something
yummy in a hurry. Tips to get
organized for speedy whole foods cooking.

Table of Contents (cont.)

(cont.)

Table of Contents (cont.)

You deserve it! American-style festive
recipes with low-stress ingredients.
Crowd pleasers and holiday fare.

Recipes:

The golden short-cuts, designed to
help you formulate a plan of action:

A concise reference guide to natural
home remedies and special healing foods

The Beginning.....

I've seen it happen again and again, in my cooking classes.

Insights sprouting up, after a tasty meal.

We plant a few new ideas in each class, before we cook.
Then, setting questions aside, we open up our senses
and join together, to explore new territory.

What is a macrobiotic diet? Why is it so effective for
self-healing? What's the most practical way to get
started?

The answers to these questions come alive when we taste.
A fresh view of life--based on eating and living in harmony
with nature, begins to take shape.

At first, the challenges seem awesome. So many new
foods to get acquainted with. Families resisting
change. Parties tempt. No time to cook.

But then, a caring friend reaches out with a supportive
gesture at just the right moment, and something takes hold.
The root sinks down....a deep, instinctively familiar
sensation wells up...and Mother Earth begins to nourish
in a totally new way. The warm milk of well-chewed food
enters and circulates with a rhythmic chant....

"I believe in my body's own regenerative powers....I can
cooperate with nature's great forces to heal myself."
Self-healing begins.

How To Read This Book

If you really want to learn to heal yourself
with food, read this book with a friend.

Do it however works best for you. Loan it,
or read it outloud together. Cook together.
Take turns cooking for each other. Challenge
each other's ideas. Get ridiculous together,
in the kitchen.

Slow down, when you taste together.
And talk about how you feel, after you eat.

Then you will know what macrobiotics is
about.

Macrobiotics: An Exciting Tool for Self-Healing

Recently, a snowballing body of scientific
research and anecdotal evidence has brought the
benefits of a macrobiotic diet into the public
attention.

A truly impressive range of symptoms can be
positively affected by a diligent application
of these dietary principles, including:

allergies
candida yeast infections
diabetes
digestive disorders
heart disease
pre-menstrual syndrome
anemia
hyperactivity in children
many types of cancer

The basic tools of macrobiotics--a wholesome,
natural diet, self-reflection, self-diagnosis skills,
and home care remedies--are simple, versatile, and
immensely practical. They evolved from the 4000 year
old traditions of Oriental medicine.

Grass-roots style, they have spread, in the past few
decades to countries all over the world. Hundreds of
thousands of people now use these tools daily, and if
you ask them why, they reply: "Because they make sense....
They work....This way of healing myself makes me feel
more alive, in control of my life, and in harmony with
nature."

In Boston, home of the Kushi Institute for macrobiotic
studies, so many folks have made the switch that both
a Howard Johnson's and a McDonalds are now offering a
macrobiotic breakfast on the menu!

The Supportive Research

Harvard Medical School
Boston's Shattuck Hospital
Tidewater Detention Center, Chesapeake, Virginia
Tulane University
University Hospital in Boston
Harvard School of Public Health
University of Minnesota School of Public Health
Boston University
New England Baptist Hospital

It's an impressive list. Harvard Med School led the way by
showing, in ten years of studies, that a macrobiotic diet may
be one of the best known ways to prevent heart disease...leading
to very low levels of cholesterol and, for Americans, unusually
low blood pressure levels.

Shattuck Hospital is preparing to publish reports on the beneficial
results of using a macrobiotic diet in the geriatrics ward,
and long-term psychiatric care ward.

Tidewater is implementing a new diet for juvenile offenders.
Infractions dropped a startling 45% merely with the removal
of sugar.

Tulane is studying the results of a macrobiotic diet with cancer
patients in the New Orleans area. The other 5 institutions
are cooperating in a team project to evaluate the progress of
700 cancer patients who have consulted with Michio Kushi in
recent years (for references, see Diet for a Strong Heart, Kushi).

A Diet For World Peace

What doesn't make the headlines is the fact that a
macrobiotic diet also calms the mind and emotions,
while renewing the body.

When this happens, something very subtle and
powerful clicks, inside. You feel more whole.

This is the kind of good news that travels
fastest by word of mouth. I'm very happy that
more and more people are arriving at my doorstep
wanting to use this diet principally to enhance
their creative potential. "I want to learn
how to eat to streamline my energy," said an
independent filmmaker.

Calm, healthy, creative people are much more likely
to resolve conflicts without violence, and much more
capable of dedicating their energies towards peaceful,
ecological living.

Many world leaders feel the message is too great
to be ignored.

At the United Nations, a Macrobiotic Society with
150 members was started by Katsuhide Katatani,
U.N. Development Director for Southeast Asia, who
healed his stomach cancer on a macrobiotic diet.
They meet regularly to discuss problems of world
health, diet, and world peace. A comparable
society is forming at UNESCO headquarters.

Locally, when a leader from a peace-action
group called BEYOND WAR came to my classes,
she said: "It's amazing, we're all learning
how to do the same work, under different names....
the work of growing more responsible for
how we live..... This food feels very right, to
me."

Macrobiotics in Perspective

Macrobiotics, however, is not a cure-all.
Nothing is.

Any healer who tells you that his methods will
absolutely cure your symptoms is a fool. If you
believe him, you're a greater fool.

Symptoms come and go.

But real healing happens when we dare to breathe in the
universe, stretching both body and soul to reach for balance
and truth. Sometimes, healing moments take forever
to arrive. At other times, they fall in our laps
with sheer grace....like a feather from an unseen
bird.

Writing this book has been my self-healing, this
past 4 years. I'm happy, finally, to be able to share
the story of my journey along the path.

My Story

One day, when I was a kid, I overheard my parents
talking. Their voices were quiet, tense, and sad,
and they were talking about one of their friends....
"in a perfect state of health"...."dropped dead of
a heart attack".

I wanted to be alone.

In the backyard, belly-down on the grass, I watched
the ants. Rolled over and looked up at the vast sky
above.

"Why, God?" I asked. So unfair, to be so alive....
and then suddenly dead, with no warning.

My own heart felt a great stillness.

Remembering it, I can still smell the green of the
grass crushed beneath me. Feel the damp of the dew
on my elbows. Hear the birdsong. My question
seemed to open up all my senses wide, in search of
an answer.

6

Years later....

With my questions still unanswered, I began to
study a succession of traditional healing arts.
Native American ceremony, western herbology, women's
folk medicine, macrobiotics, and shiatsu. I lived for a
year at the Findhorn Community, in the north of Scotland,
where I discovered the magic of cooking with spirit.

With each new field I explored, I felt that same
hush enter my heart.

And after the quiet, a growing feeling that the
earth was speaking to me, through my senses.

I learned that if we listen closely with all our senses,
our bodies <u>do</u> warn us when illness is coming. And, we can
take steps <u>to</u> prevent that illness, right in our own kitchens.

With relief, that place in my heart that had
stood still since childhood began to breathe again,
rejoice, and spill over.

Eventually, it started to keep me awake, all hours
of the night, demanding, with a louder and louder
inner voice, that I write down what I've learned,
so you can benefit by it, too.

And that, dear reader, is how this cookbook came to be.

Kristina Turner
December, 1987
Grass Valley, California

7

My Heartfelt Thanks

Thanks, first, to Rich, for helping me bring
this book down to earth. His gentle wit and
wisdom so often lit the way home.

"We take a step, then we stumble," Rich told me.
"The joy in life comes when we make a dance
out of both."

What could be more ridiculous--and full of steps
and stumbles--than trying to change our lifelong
food habits in a matter of weeks? Yet we did.

In 1979, when my husband Rich Turner faced mysterious health
symptoms which defied both diagnosis and cure, we turned to
macrobiotics. I will always be grateful for the renewed
strength, vitality, and joy we found on this path.

Yet in March 1989, Rich died peacefully, with a rare
form of cancer. A loving circle of friends gathered round
in his last hours to say goodbye. All agreed his passing
felt deeply healing--more like a birth than a death.

Thanks to all my family and friends, and especially to
Shira, Mim, Sharon, Steve, Kate, Emile, Betty and Nan,
for the nurture, clear counsel, and practical support
that has helped me to stay grounded and open my heart
through times of profound change.

And my very special thanks to Matthew, who has journeyed
with me through passion, parenting, and publishing--seeking
beyond illusion for the truth that heals.

Finally, thanks to you reader. For taking
time to read between the lines and discover
your own truth.

These are exciting times to be alive.
Healing ourselves, healing our Earth.
I'm glad we are here, together.

Kristina Turner
December, 2002
Vashon, Washington

1 Getting Started With Basics

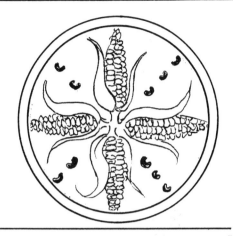

Everybody has minor symptoms. Aches and pains, tension, upset stomachs, headaches, skin eruptions, mood swings, occasional colds and flu. Some of us have a constant stream of these, lucky others just a rare twinge.

A self-healing lifestyle starts with recognizing that minor symptoms don't just happen to us. We have an active hand in creating them, by the choices we make in our daily lives.

How we exercise, how we cope with stress, what we eat. All of these contribute to our bodies' natural ability to maintain equilibrium and health. Especially how we eat.

But the truth is, most of us don't want to make changes in our diets, just for the sake of healing minor symptoms.... unless they start to happen too frequently. Or, until they escalate into bigger symptoms.

The shock of a high-blood-cholesterol reading. Chronic, worrisome overweight, fatigue, or allergies. Sudden startling pain, or embarrassing loss of agility, memory, or consciousness.

These are terrible motivators. We shudder to think of what may come next....knowing full well that the diseases of aging in our high-stress, polluted society are often painful and debilitating.

Whether you have only minor symptoms, or more troubling, persistent ones, you've probably been prompted to open this book by a nagging inner question: "Isn't there something I can do?"

There is something you can do. And this chapter gives you the tools to get started.....Three basic principles from macrobiotics shed light on why illness happens, and point towards renewing daily food choices which can begin to bring your body into a new state of balance.

Basic Self-Healing Principles

#1   EAT IN HARMONY WITH NATURE

* Traditional, whole, unrefined foods

* Primarily locally grown

* Cooked appropriately for each season

#2 BALANCE NATURAL FORCES IN COOKING

Seeking a healthful blend of:
* warm and cool
* wet and dry
* heavy and light
* hard and soft
* salty and sweet
* quick and slow
* ordinary and inspired!

#3 USE FOOD TO CREATE DESIRED EFFECTS...

* In your body
* In your moods
* In your life

← calm, healthy kid

Principle #1: Eat in Harmony With Nature

Sometimes I think our ancestors would laugh through their tears if they could see how we eat.

In the past two hundred years, since the advent of modern agricultural and food processing techniques, our diet has progressively gotten farther and farther away from the natural foods which sustained traditional peoples all over the earth for centuries...primarily whole grains, beans, locally grown vegetables and fruits, and small quantities of fish and sea vegetables, wild and range-fed animals, and natural condiments.

Instead, we eat mostly from colorful boxes and cans. We spray our vegetables and fruits with deadly chemicals, then ship them half-way around the world before we eat them. We keep chickens awake with electric lights, and feed them hormones to get them to lay eggs constantly.

It's been a grand experiment in the wonders of technology.... but what a price we're paying in our health!

UNNATURAL MODERN DIET TRENDS INCLUDE:

1. High consumption of animal foods
   (meat, poultry, eggs, and dairy)

2. Junk Foods (high in sugar, chemicals, fat, refined salt, and hype)

3. More mechanized food (frozen, spun, hydrogenated, microwaved, etc.)

In traditional societies eating a more natural diet, many modern degenerative diseases were almost non-existant, including:

* Heart disease
* Cancer
* Osteoporosis
* Diabetes
* Hypertension

Volumes of scientific research are now documenting the clear connection between our modern, devitalized diet, and the rise of these diseases in every westernized country (see

books by Ballentine, McDougall, Kushi, and Pritikin
for highly readable and informative overviews of
this research).

A Return to Nature Can Heal

Nature designed our bodies to be self-regulating, self-
renewing organisms that respond wisely and sensitively
to the ever-changing world around us.

Many scientific experiments have now demonstrated that
if we simply return to eating more traditional, natural
foods, the body often begins to heal itself. For example:

FOR DIABETES: McDougall reports that at the University
of Kentucky, investigators found that
approximately 75% of patients in a study
of adult-onset diabetes were freed from
their need for insulin medication after
only a few weeks of changing to a high-
carbohydrate, low-fat, high-fiber diet
(The McDougall Plan, John McDougall, M.D.).

FOR HEART DISEASE: Kushi reports that researchers at Harvard
Medical School have good news for prevention
of heart disease... Control groups of
macrobiotic, natural food eaters were
found to have very low blood pressure
and cholesterol readings. When placed
for 1 month on a diet containing 250 g.
of beef, these levels rose significantly.
Within 2 weeks of discontinuing the beef,
cholesterol and blood pressure returned
to unusual low levels (Diet for a Strong
Heart, Michio Kushi).

TO PREVENT SERIOUS ILLNESS

And/or help your body heal persistent
symptoms, here's two of the smartest
things you can do:

1] Eat more traditional, natural meals

2] Cut down on modern, high-stress foods

Traditional Meals

Originally, in Old English, the word "meal" meant grain.

Meals based on whole grains and vegetables were, in fact, the staple fare world-wide long before meat and potatoes became the standard Western supper.

Of course, Eskimos, American pioneers, and other migratory peoples relied on meat when food-growing was impractical. But, wherever people settled down to grow crops and build lasting civilizations, they discovered how versatile grains can be:

CRACKED and cooked as cereal
GROUND INTO FLOUR for bread, tortillas, pancakes
DRIED AS PASTA for spaghetti, lasagna, soba noodles
COOKED WHOLE and served alongside stews, stir-fries, or beans
LEFTOVER, TOSSED IN SALAD with crisp vegetables & seafood
ROLLED UP INSIDE knishes, sushi, burritos, cabbage rolls

Modern nutritional analysis confirms that the typical ingredients in our ancestors' grain-based meals added up to a balanced, health-promoting diet:

Traditional Nutrition

BASIC FOODS	% of DIET	PROVIDE THESE ESSENTIALS:
Grains & Vegetables	75-80%	Complex carbohydrates, fiber, protein, fat, Vit A, B, C, E, iron, calcium
Soup	5%	Warming stimulation for good digestion
Beans, Fish, Occasional Seeds, Nuts, Meat, Eggs, and Dairy	5-10%	Ample protein and fat, added calcium, iron, B vitamins
Varied Extras:	5-10%	
Sea Vegetables -		Calcium, iron, vitamins, trace minerals
Seasonal Fruits -		Carbohydrates, fiber, vitamins & minerals
Fermented foods (miso, yogurt, etc.) -		Live enzymes to aid digestion, Vit B_{12}
Herbs & Spices -		Appetite stimulation, trace nutrients

Eating By Nature's Design

However, more than tradition points towards
the wisdom of eating whole grains and vegetables
as our principle food.

Nature's design for us is revealed by a
common sense look at our physical structure:

OUR TEETH
are built to grind mostly high-
fiber foods such as whole grains,
seeds, leafy greens and roots.
20 out of 32 teeth are grinding
molars.

INTERNAL
ORGANS
function very smoothly on a grain,
bean, and vegetable diet. Complex
carbohydrates regulate blood-sugar
and provide steady energy.

But on a diet rich in fat, protein,
sugar, and salt, organs such as
kidneys, liver, gall bladder, and
heart often become weak and clogged,
depleting our vitality and leading
to illness.

INTESTINES
are self-regulating and cleansing
on a high-fiber diet. But a typical
American low-fiber diet leads to
sluggishness, gas, and susceptibility
to colon cancer.

HELPFUL
BACTERIA
thrive in our intestines on a grain-
based diet. But these die off and
are replaced by unhealthy micro-
organisms when we eat too much fat,
sugar, meat, or chemicals. Fermented
foods help to renew the healthy
bacteria population.

HEALTHY
BLOOD
flows freely on a low-fat, low-sweet diet.
High fat meals, by contrast, make blood
thick and sludgy. Sugar weakens and
thins the blood.

WHOLE GRAINS EVOLVED ON THE PLANET AT THE SAME
TIME AS HUMAN BEINGS....

Modern, High-Stress Foods

TOO MANY OF THESE FOODS	CAN HAVE THESE STRESSFUL EFFECTS:	CUT DOWN, TO PREVENT:
<u>FATS</u> Dairy food Fatty meats Fried foods Nuts, etc. 	- Harden arteries - Form excess mucus - Cloud thinking - Congest & impede function of heart, liver, gall bladder, lungs, intestines & sexual organs	High Blood Pressure Food Allergies Heart Disease Diabetes Eating Disorders Colon & Other Cancers
<u>SWEETS</u> Sugar Honey Molasses Corn Syrup Artificial sweets Chocolate 	- Cause blood sugar imbalances & hyperactivity - Overwork spleen, pancreas, liver & intestines - Cause mood swings, irritability & fatigue - Lower resistance to infection	Hypoglycemia Diabetes Emotional Hysteria Eating Disorders Reproductive & Other Cancers
<u>HIGH-PROTEIN</u> <u>ANIMAL FOODS</u> Red Meat Pork Eggs, etc. 	- Toxify & acidify blood - Deplete supply of calcium - Overwork kidney & liver - Stagnate in intestines, killing intestinal flora	Kidney Stones Liver Disease Colon & Reproductive Cancers Arthritis Osteoporosis

STAPLE GRAINS AROUND THE WORLD

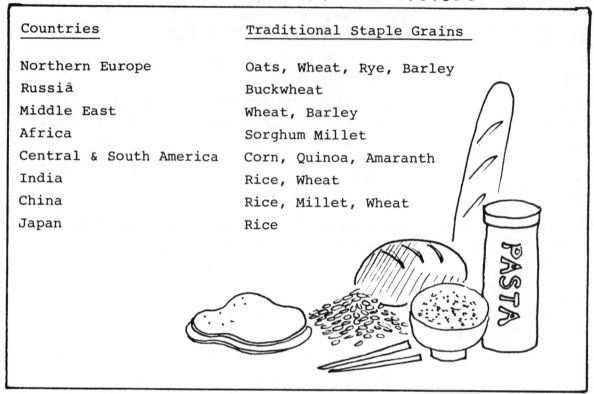

Countries	Traditional Staple Grains
Northern Europe	Oats, Wheat, Rye, Barley
Russia	Buckwheat
Middle East	Wheat, Barley
Africa	Sorghum Millet
Central & South America	Corn, Quinoa, Amaranth
India	Rice, Wheat
China	Rice, Millet, Wheat
Japan	Rice

Natural Weight Loss

One of the most commonly asked questions in my cooking classes
is: "How can I lose weight on a diet so high in grains?....
Aren't they fattening?"

To answer this question, it's important first to correct a
common misconception. Whole grains are <u>not</u> fattening.
people all over the planet rely on whole grains as their
primary food, and yet most of the world's people aren't
overweight.

Most Americans <u>are</u> overweight, and we eat a diet which is
very low in whole grains, but contains over 40% fat and
approximately 20% sugars. Grains are not the problem.

What misleads most weight-watchers is that grains are
moderately high in calories. But, unlike high-caloric
fatty and sugary foods, whole grains are nutrition-rich.
Packed with vitamins, minerals, energy-sustaining carbohydrates,
protein, and cleansing fiber, they are a complete food.

As a result, when you eat more whole grains daily,
you feel full more quickly, and satisfied long after eating.
Conventional "diet" foods--such as salads, or no-cal sodas--
by contrast, always leave you hungry for more.

Nutrient Sources in Whole Foods

COMPLEX CARBOHYDRATES:	Whole grains, beans, vegetables, fruits
PROTEIN:	Beans, fish, seeds, nuts, whole grains, seaweeds
FAT:	Seeds, nuts, oils, beans, fish, tofu, tempeh, oats
CALCIUM:	Dark greens (kale, collards, etc.), soybeans, seaweeds, seeds
IRON:	Dark greens, seaweeds, millet, lentil, garbanzo beans, seeds
VIT. A:	Dark leafy greens, carrots, squashes, seaweeds
B VITAMINS:	Whole grains, sea vegetables, lentils, fish, fermented foods
VIT. B_{12}:	Small amounts of fish, grain-fed poultry, meat, eggs or dairy
VIT. C:	Dark greens (kale, parsley, broccoli, etc.), local fruits
VIT. E:	Whole grains, unrefined oils, seeds, leafy greens
TRACE MINERALS:	Sea salt, seaweeds, organic produce

The fact, is, most people can eat their fill and lose weight when they begin to follow the 3 Basic Principles in this chapter. "I'm so happy I can look in the mirror now, and know I don't have to worry about weight....I'm enjoying food, losing pounds steadily, and I understand why!" said a recent student.

For more specific guidelines on Losing Weight Naturally, see pp. 176-181.

In Summary

Throughout history, human beings have thrived on a diet of whole, natural foods. Many degenerative illnesses are on the increase as a result of our modern shift towards processed foods high in FAT, SALT, SUGAR & CHEMICALS.

3 BASIC PRINCIPLES can guide you towards a whole foods diet that restores your body's natural, self-healing abilities. (Principle #1 is covered here, in detail. For #2 and 3, turn to the next chapter):

1. EAT IN HARMONY WITH NATURE
2. BALANCE NATURE"S FORCES IN COOKING
3. USE FOOD TO CREATE DESIRED EFFECTS

Now, for practicalities! This chapter concludes with Self-Healing Diet Guidelines, Basic Recipes for Getting Started, a Starter Shopping List, and a relaxing visualization exercise to help you tune-in to your body's special needs.

Self-Healing Diet Guidelines

The Path Starts Here....

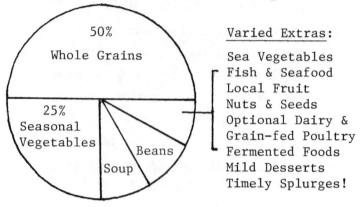

50%
Whole Grains

25%
Seasonal
Vegetables

Beans

Soup

Varied Extras:

Sea Vegetables
Fish & Seafood
Local Fruit
Nuts & Seeds
Optional Dairy &
Grain-fed Poultry
Fermented Foods
Mild Desserts
Timely Splurges!

Foods to Minimize:

Sugar & Honey
Artificial Foods
Fats (meat, dairy, oil)
White Flour
Refined Salt
Pesticides
Ice Cold Food & Drinks
Alcohol, Caffeine
Drugs

1. Learn from traditional peoples. They ate hearty,
    sustaining meals, high in complex carbohydrates. To
    get started on a healing diet, try the proportions in
    the diagram above. This will give you a healthy balance
    of carbohydrates and protein, with minimal fat.
    (For calcium and Vitamin C, include dark leafy greens).

2. Experiment for 1-3 months. Cook a variety of whole
    meals. Enjoy low-guilt desserts (see p. 147). Take
    time to chew. Notice how each meal makes you feel.
    Then, take a breather. It's OK to go back to your old
    ways. (We all do, in cycles!). Your body and moods
    will let you know when you need to return to the
    simple pleasures of whole, natural foods.

3. Stay flexible, with the changing seasons. When the
    weather turns warm, cook less grain and eat more pasta,
    veggies, and fruit. When the cold comes, eat more
    pressure-cooked grains, roots, and hearty bean soups
    (see pp. 54-64 for tips on seasonal cooking).

4. Study, and ask questions. Learn to cook for your changing
    needs. If you're pregnant or nursing, for example, you
    need foods high in calcium and Vitamin B-12 (see pp. 118,
    191). If you live in a city, you may need more animal
    food, to buffer yourself from stress. But a move to the
    country could prompt you to eat less animal food, and
    re-sensitize yourself to Nature with more garden veggies.

    You'll know when it's time, my friend, to go beyond
    these guidelines. Trust your instincts.

Basic Recipes for Getting Started

BASIC GRAINS

Pot-boiled rice
Pressure cooked brown rice
Rice with Fun Extras
Millet
Buckwheat
Hot Cereals
Quick Pilafs
Corn Polenta

SESAME SALT

MISO SOUP

HEARTY BEANS

Aduki
Lentil
Gingered black beans
Garbanzo beans

For your first meals, keep it simple. For breakfast, try a hot cereal, or miso soup and whole-grain toast.

Reward yourself by eating lunch out...

Then, for a hearty dinner, serve brown rice, millet, or bulghur pilaf, topped with sesame salt, a side of beans, and steamed leafy greens or salad.

Cook enough for tomorrow's lunch (try the recipe for Sesame-Rice Burritos on p. 103). In later chapters, these Basics will appear as leftovers, in everything from rice salad and bean spread, to creamy soups, burgers, cookies and pudding!

For your convenience, a Starter Shopping List and relaxing visualization conclude the chapter.

Basic Grains

Pot Boiled Brown Rice

1 c. brown rice (short or
 long grain or brown basmati)
2 c. boiling water
pinch sea salt

Larger batches, less water:
3 c. rice / 5½ c. water

Wash the rice by swirling it in
a bowl of cool water. Drain in a
large, fine-mesh strainer (pat to
remove excess water). Then place
in a pot with a snug-fitting lid.
Add water & salt, bring to a boil,
cover and simmer--without stirring,
without lifting the lid--for 50-60
minutes. Relax...dinner is
cooking itself.

Pressure-Cooked Brown Rice

2 c. short grain brown rice
3 - 3½ c. water
1/8 tsp. sea salt

FUN EXTRAS:

For playful variety, soak ¼ c.
of one of these in ½ c. water
for 3-4 hours, then cook it
with your rice:

rye or wheat berries
barley
wild rice
sweet brown rice
dried chestnuts

"So nutty and delicious," is the
chorus from my cooking students.
"Doesn't even need butter!"
Pressure cooking makes rice
delectably chewy,* aromatic, and
very digestable. Holds in flavor,
and vitamins, too.

DIRECTIONS: Wash the rice and
drain in a strainer (as in recipe
above). Place in pressure cooker
with water and salt, and start on
medium-low heat for 20 minutes.
Then, turn to high briefly until
pressure valve jiggles. Put a
flame spreader under the pot, to
keep from burning rice on the
bottom. Turn to simmer and cook
40 minutes more (1 hour total).

*Texture tips: If too sticky, use
slightly less water; if too dry, or
bottom browns, add a little more water
to your next pot of rice. Cook plenty--
it reheats easily in a vegetable steamer!

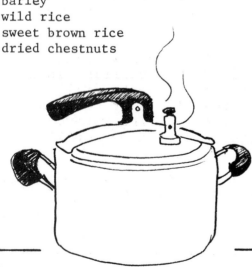

Millet

Pot-Boiled:

1 c. millet
3 c. water
pinch sea salt

Pressure Cooked:

2 c. millet
5 c. water
pinch sea salt

For variety, add:

1 c. winter squash
(peeled & cubed)
1 small onion
1 c. water

Or, 1 c. diced cabbage,
cauliflower or carrot
½ c. water

Millet's cheerful color and mild flavor make it a tasty breakfast grain. Or, cook it with vegetables and serve with saucy beans for supper.

Wash millet, and drain in a strainer. For the fluffiest texture and best flavor, dry roast in a skillet by stirring over medium heat until it smells toasty. Meanwhile, bring water to a boil. Add millet and salt, cover and simmer 25 minutes.

To pressure cook, place roasted millet and water in the cooker. Bring to pressure on high heat, then turn to simmer and cook 25 minutes. Especially tasty cooked with winter squash and onion.

Buckwheat

1 c. raw buckwheat
(not roasted groats)
2 c. water
very small pinch sea salt

Variations:

Add 1/2 c. extra water
plus 1 c. of diced
cabbage,
cauliflower
or onion

The heartiest grain...best in cold weather, or if you're feeling low energy.

Dry roast (don't bother washing, it gets too sticky), by stirring in a skillet over medium heat until it browns. For the fluffiest texture, add gradually to boiling water, quickly cover, and simmer for 20 minutes.

Delicious with Sesame Gravy (p. 164), or steamed, mashed winter squash.

Hot Cereals

Cracked Wheat & Rye

1/2 c. cracked wheat
1/2 c. cracked rye
4 c. water
1/8 tsp. sea salt

To bring out the best flavor in the cracked grain, dry roast it in a skillet, by stirring over medium heat until it smells nutty--but don't brown. Then, sprinkle into water, while stirring to avoid lumps. Add salt, bring to a boil, cover and simmer 30-40 minutes (put a flame spreader under the pot, to keep it from sticking). The longer it cooks, the better it tastes! For variety, substitute cracked barley, buckwheat, or brown rice.

Overnight Oats

3/4 c. whole oat groats
1/4 c. brown rice
1 pinch sea salt
4 c. water

Low-Fat Alternative:

Use half rice,
half oats

Our foremothers used to make this hearty cereal on the woodstove--leaving it overnight to simmer gently. To approximate the same effect, bring oats and rice to a boil, cover and simmer 5 minutes, then turn off heat and let sit overnight. Plan to wake up early the next morning, bring the pot to a boil, stir and add a little water, if needed, for desired creaminess....then, put a flame spreader underneath and let simmer 45 minutes to an hour.

Want a Yummy Non-Dairy Alternative to Milk on Your Cereal?

Try Almond or Sunflower Milk, (p. 99).

And for optional sweetness, top with a spoonful of brown rice syrup.

Quick Pilafs

Bulghur Wheat

1 c. bulghur
2 c. water
pinch sea salt

Onion Pilaf Variation:

1 tsp. toasted sesame oil
1 onion, sliced thinly
2 T. sesame or sunflower
seeds
1 tsp. tamari soy sauce

Pour boiling water over bulghur and salt and simmer, covered, for 20 minutes....or, cover and let soak for an hour until it gets fluffy.

For Onion Pilaf, saute onion in sesame oil, stirring until golden and translucent. Add bulghur and seeds. Saute briefly, then pour in water and bring to a boil. Cover and simmer 20 minutes. Season with tamari to taste.

Quinoa

1 c. quinoa
2¼ c. water
pinch sea salt

Variation:

Add diced onion,
or
3 T. sesame or
sunflower seeds

Wonderfully fluffy, light, and filling, quinoa (pronounced keen-wa) was the staple grain of Incan civilizations. Just recently available in this country. I think it's rich nutty flavor will soon make it popular, even though it costs more than most other grains.

To cook, roast in a skillet, stirring until nutty smelling. Add to boiling water, cover and simmer 20 minutes.

Tangy Rice Pilaf

2 c. leftover brown rice
½ onion, sliced
1 c. cabbage, diced
1 umeboshi plum, pitted

3/4 c. water

Make this for a quick supper out of yesterday's leftover rice.

Mince the umeboshi plum (a tangy pickled plum, well-known in the Orient as a digestive aid). Spread it in a skillet, add vegetables, then lay rice on top. Pour in water, bring to a boil, and simmer, covered 5-8 minutes--until cabbage is tender. Tumble and serve.

Our Native Grain

Corn Polenta

1 c. coarse ground corn meal

3 c. water

1/4 c. water

1/4 tsp. sea salt

Roast cornmeal by stirring in
a skillet over medium heat
until it smells sweet. Place
in a heavy pot. Pour boiling
water over it and stir very
quickly to dissolve any lumps.
It will start to thicken in a
few minutes--then use a spoon to
pull mush away from the side of the pan
while you pour in 1/4 c. water (don't stir it in--
this keeps the mush from sticking to the sides).
Simmer, covered, for 45 to an hour. Flavor gets
better the longer you cook it.

Fried Cornmeal Mush: For a treat, make polenta the night before,
chill, slice, and saute in sesame oil. Serve with maple syrup
or unsweetened apple butter.

Sesame Salt

1 c. unhulled, brown sesame seeds

1 to 2 tsp. unrefined sea salt

Roast seeds, by stirring in a skillet over medium-low
heat until they smell toasty and crumble easily between
thumb and forefinger. If using moist sea salt, lightly
roast it, then add to seeds and grind in a suribachi
(Japanese mortar & pestle), until mostly crumbled.
Store in a sealed jar in the fridge.

Miso Soup

Cool Weather Soup:

2½ c. water
½ c. sliced carrot
½ c. sliced kale or watercress
1 green onion, sliced fine
3" strip wakame seaweed
1 T. barley miso (2 year,
unpasteurized variety)

Warm Weather Variations:

Substitute juicier vegetables--
chinese cabbage, fresh corn,
radishes, green beans, or
crookneck squash. Try a lighter
miso--such as low-salt Chick Pea
Miso.

Cut a 3" strip of wakame into
small pieces (use scissors, or
soak, then slice with a knife).
Bring water to a boil, add wakame
and carrot, and simmer 15 minutes.
Add kale and cook 5 minutes,
then add green onion and simmer
briefly. Turn off the heat,
and dissolve miso into the soup
by stirring it through a
strainer.

The Miso Story

Miso is a savory, fermented flavoring paste made
from soybeans and/or grains and sea salt. It's been
honored for centuries in China and Japan as a healing
food, and modern nutrition research reveals why....

A good source of protein and B vitamins, miso
also helps to cleanse radiation and nicotene
from the body. Unpasteurized miso contains
friendly bacterial enzymes which can rebuild
intestinal flora that get destroyed on a diet
high in meat, sugar, chemicals and antibiotics.

However, if you have candida yeast infection,
experiment with miso cautiously (see The Yeast
Connection, William Crook, M.D.). In some people
miso helps combat the yeast, in others makes
it worse (especially try chickpea and hatcho miso).

For restricted sodium diet, add just 1/4 tsp. miso
to your soup, and you'll still reap the benefits of live
enzymes. For low-salt, try American Miso Co. brand.

MISO VARIETIES

Barley - rich flavor

Mellow - sweet & salty

Chickpea - mild & sweet

Hatcho - hearty & savory

Hearty Beans

Four beans are used most often in macrobiotic cooking: aduki, lentil, garbanzo, and black beans. These are lowest in fats, and native to a temperate climate.

Aduki and lentils are especially handy, because they don't need soaking. Seaweeds are included in these recipes because they soften the beans and speed cooking time, as well as providing a wealth of nutrients--calcium, iron, B vitamins, and trace minerals.

Aduki Beans

1 c. aduki beans
4 c. water
1 strip kombu seaweed
¼ - ½ tsp. sea salt

Sweet Variation: Add 1 c. butternut squash (peeled & diced), the last half-hour of cooking.

Wash beans and place in a pot with kombu and half the water. Bring to a boil, cover and simmer ½ hour. Then pour in the rest of the cold water-- this 'shocks' the beans, making them soften and cook faster. Simmer another hour, or until beans are tender. Add salt the last 10 minutes. Adukis, by the way, are the least gas-forming bean.

Lentils

1 c. lentils
3" strip wakame seaweed
1 onion, diced
water to cover
¼ - ½ tsp. sea salt
or, 1 T. tamari soy sauce

Wash lentils, soak and slice the wakame in small pieces, then place together in pot, with onion. Add water to cover, bring to a boil, cover the pot and simmer 45 minutes. Add water as needed, for the consistency you want. Add salt or tamari the last 10 minutes.

HEARTY LENTIL STEW

Add 2 c. root vegetables (carrot, parsnip, onion, rutabega, burdock, etc.) to the basic lentil recipe above. Add ½ c. sliced kale, celery, or watercress the last 10 minutes. Season with bay leaf or thyme, and tamari.

Gingered Black Beans

1½ c. black turtle beans
4 c. water
1 strip kombu
2 tsp. tamari soy sauce
1 tsp. finely grated ginger

The Queen of Beans...makes her own rich, velvet sauce. Elegant soul food for a wedding or a picnic!

Sort beans for rocks, then wash and soak overnight. Place in pressure cooker and boil uncovered 5 minutes. Skim off foam. Add kombu, cover and bring to pressure, then cook 1½ hours. Bring down from pressure, add tamari and ginger, and simmer 10 minutes. (To pot-boil, simmer 2-3 hours until tender, adding water as needed for a saucy gravy). These taste even better the next day.

Garbanzo Beans

1 c. garbanzo beans
(also called chickpeas)
3 c. water
1 strip kombu seaweed
¼ tsp. sea salt

Check beans for rocks, then wash and soak. If you tend to get gas from beans, discard soaking water and add fresh. Place in pressure cooker and boil uncovered for 5 minutes. Skim off any foam. Add kombu, cover, and bring to pressure. Simmer 45 minutes. Bring down from pressure, add salt, and simmer 10 minutes more.

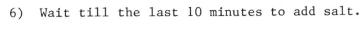

To Soften Beans + Avoid Gas...

1) Overnight soak all beans larger than aduki.

2) To minimize gas...discard soaking water and add fresh.

3) Pressure-cook big beans--makes them extra tender.

4) Cook uncovered the first 10 minutes & skim off foam.

5) Cook together with kombu seaweed--a natural tenderizer.

6) Wait till the last 10 minutes to add salt.

Starter Shopping List

Now, take a deep breath and relax. The most lasting changes
happen gradually. One step at a time.

This basic shopping list can help you stock your cupboards
for many of the recipes in this book. Most of these foods
are widely available at health food stores. But if you can't
find a particular one, you can order by mail (see Resources,
p. 206).

Whole Grains & Grain Products

brown rice
(short grain)
millet
whole oats
barley
bulghar wheat
buckwheat

buckwheat noodles
whole wheat elbows

Fresh, Seasonal Vegetables

dark, leafy greens (see p. 55)

Beans & Soyfoods

aduki beans
lentils
garbanzo beans
black beans
tofu (perishable)
tempeh (keeps frozen

Sea Vegetables

kombu (for beans)
wakame (for soup)
agar agar (for jello)
See Chapter 6 for more

Condiments, Seeds & Nuts

tamari soy sauce (also called shoyu)
sea salt
miso (dark, unpasteurized barley type)
sesame oil
fresh ginger root
brown rice vinegar
natural sauerkraut
natural mustard
kuzu (a thickener for sauces)
umeboshi plums
sesame seeds
sunflower seeds
pumpkin seeds
almonds
walnuts

Whole Grain Breads

corn tortillas
whole wheat chapati
whole wheat pita
unyeasted sourdough breads
(the most digestable)
sprouted grain breads

Spreads & Jams

unsweetened apple butter
fruit-only jams (read labels)
toasted sesame butter
toasted almond butter

Fruits & Sweeteners

fresh local fruit
dried local fruit
brown rice syrup
barley malt syrup
apple juice
maple syrup

Beverages

spring water
grain coffee-substitutes
roasted barley tea
kukicha twig tea (see Healing Foods Glossary, p. 199)
apple juice (for fun, mix with
   sparkling water)
mild herb teas, such as:
   raspberry leaf
   red clover
   nettles
   chamomile

Breakfast Cereals

puffed rice, wheat, corn
corn & wheat flakes
   (barley malt sweetened)
granola with barley malt
cracked grain cereals
polenta
rolled oats

SNACKS

Crunchy:

baked brown rice crackers
rye crisp
rice cakes
toasted seeds

Chewy:

popcorn
mochi (a rice snack that puffs
   when you bake it--very chewy)
unyeasted rye or wheat breads

Sweet:

Essene sprouted breads
raisins
amasake (a creamy sweet, fermented
   rice beverage--like a malt!)
yinnies rice syrup candies

Talk To Your Body:
A Guided Visualization

Here's a simple exercise you can use whenever
your mind feels saturated with new information
about diet! It can help you tune-in to your
own body's innate wisdom...and get clear
about the next steps in self-healing.

1. Begin by sitting quietly, in a
    comfortable chair.

2. Relax....let your body sink down
    into the chair....giving your
    weight to the earth. Notice how
    you are breathing...and gradually
    let it get deeper and more even.

3. Now, in your imagination, go
    inside your body. Look for any
    place that feels uncomfortable, or
    in need of special, loving attention.
    Talk to it, like you would talk
    to a friend....

    "Hi there, can I help? What do
    you need?" Listen for an answer.

4. Ask it to tell you, or show you a
    picture of how it <u>wants</u> to feel.

5. Now, get a sense of a particular
    food that would make your body feel
    both calm and energized. Is there
    a new food it wants to try this
    week? Or a familiar food that
    would be especially vitalizing?

When you have an answer, say thanks! Open your eyes, and
decide how and when you want to cook your "healing food".
Finally, savor it. Just <u>one</u> food, eaten in a spirit of
cooperating with your body's intuitive needs, may be the most
important first step you take towards gaining greater control
of your health.

2 New Eating Habits for Balanced Living

Your body and your lifestyle are unique.
There is no one else quite like you in the universe.

To keep your body in a state of healthy balance, it makes sense that your diet also needs to be unique.

That's why most diet plans, which have Recommended Menus intended for every reader, don't work.

Thinking for yourself, however, does work.

To help you plan the most healing meals, this chapter takes an in-depth look at Self-Healing Principles #2 and 3:

2]   BALANCE NATURAL FORCES IN COOKING

3]   USE FOOD TO CREATE DESIRED EFFECTS IN YOUR LIFE

It's a fresh approach to diet and healing.

Ask a friend to read these ideas, too....and discuss them over a shared meal.

You may discover, as I have, that new eating habits thrive best in the company of friends who understand our motives for change.

Touch a friend with your self-healing story.
Look for answers together.

The circle will widen.

Principle #2: Balance Nature's Forces in Cooking

All life on earth is busy balancing two complementary/
opposite natural forces: expansion and contraction
(known in the Orient as yin and yang).

Contraction holds our bodies together, in a dense,
compact mass. Gravity is the strongest contractive force.

Expansive forces, such as centrifugality, pull against
gravity to create the atmosphere all around us, enabling
us to breathe, move around, think, and feel.

To stay in good health, our bodies need to keep both forces
in balance.

The food we eat everyday is a major contributing factor
in whether or not our bodies and moods become too loose,
expanded, and ungrounded, or too tight, heavy, and contracted.

The next several charts can help you determine how an
excess of expansive or contractive foods, or both, may
be contributing to your recurring moods and health symptoms.

 EXPANSIVE FOODS

light, porous
usually grow upwards
perishable
grow in warm climate
tender, juicy
cool, wet
raw
sweet, sour, or bitter
spicy or oily
chemically processed

FUEL:

mental, psychological,
or spiritual activity
relaxation, looseness

 CONTRACTIVE FOODS

dense, heavy
usually grow downwards
keep well
grow in cool climate
tough, fibrous
warm, dry
cooked
salty, bland, or meaty

FUEL:

physical activity
purposefulness
focused work, tension

The Balance Chart

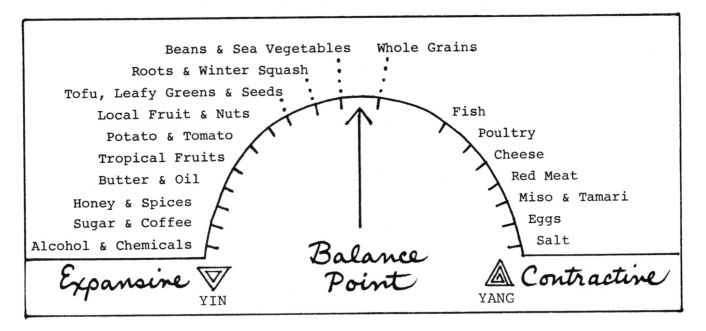

Beans & Sea Vegetables   Whole Grains

Roots & Winter Squash

Tofu, Leafy Greens & Seeds

Local Fruit & Nuts   Fish

Potato & Tomato   Poultry

Tropical Fruits   Cheese

Butter & Oil   Red Meat

Honey & Spices   Miso & Tamari

Sugar & Coffee   Eggs

Alcohol & Chemicals   Salt

Expansive ▽ YIN   Balance Point   △ YANG Contractive

HOW TO EAT FOR BALANCE

1. Your body has a natural urge for balance.

2. Notice how foods on one extreme of this chart often
    create cravings for the other extreme, to balance you.

3. Or, you may notice you mostly crave foods on only one
    side of the chart. Do you eat these to balance other
    factors in your life? (Coffee and donuts, candy and
    soda pop, for example, are routinely used to break up
    the daily grind at work!). See The Inner Balance Exercise,
    p. 87, for a gentle way to bring yourself back to center.

4. A steady diet of extreme foods can lead to mood swings
    and serious physical symptoms.

5. A steady diet of foods in the middle (from local fruit
    to fish), renews energy, relieves stress, and prevents
    many illnesses.

    (To learn how cooking methods also create balance,
    see p. 63).

The Food-Mood Connection

Eating on the extremes throws both your body and moods off balance.

One of the easiest ways to evaluate if your diet is too expansive or contractive is to listen to your moods. Are your moods too expanded, too contracted, or do you swing between both?

TOO EXPANDED (Yin)

Too much sugar, chocolate, alcohol, fruit, etc. can make you feel briefly elated & energized, then:

spaced out, dreamy
confused, forgetful
worried, sad
overly sensitive
no will power
silly, helpless, scared
hyperactive, drunk
hysterical

TOO CONTRACTED (Yang)

Too much salt, meat, cheese, or eggs can make you feel aggressive & competitive, then:

impatient, frustrated
stubborn, resentful
heavy, stuck
insensitive
compulsive, driven
controlling
angry
violent

Breaking the Food Craving Cycle

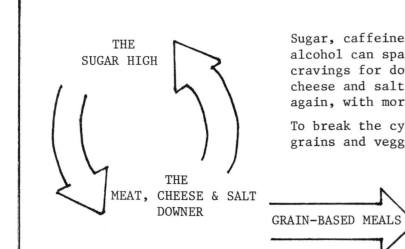

THE
SUGAR HIGH

THE
MEAT, CHEESE & SALT
DOWNER

GRAIN-BASED MEALS

Sugar, caffeine, tropical fruits & alcohol can space you out and lead to cravings for down-to-earth meat, eggs, cheese and salt....then, up you go again, with more sugar, chocolate, etc.

To break the cycle, eat more whole grains and veggies.....

NEW BALANCE

* Steady energy
* Fewer cravings
* Less dramatic moods

The Food-Symptom Link

Extreme foods also contribute to yin and yang symptoms (over-expanded or over-contracted).

Just imagine what would happen if you ate only fruit, ice cream, and coffee for 6 months. Would you feel chilled? Have loose bowels? What else?....Now, imagine the opposite. Cheese, eggs and salt for 6 months. Would you be tense? Constipated?....

Look below to see if your most common symptoms indicate that your diet has been too yin, too yang, or both:

YIN SYMPTOMS

dull, lingering aches & pains
moist conditions (runny nose,
  loose bowels, etc.)
symptoms in front of body or head
feel chilled or mildly feverish
fatigue, muscle weakness
difficulty breathing in
bruise easily

YANG SYMPTOMS

sudden sharp pains
dry conditions (rough skin,
  hard bowel movements, etc.)
symptoms in back of body or head
sudden, high fever
muscle tension
difficulty breathing out
toss & turn at night, grind teeth

To Relieve Minor Symptoms*

Cut down on extremes. Eat more foods in the middle of the Balance Chart. Then, if needed adjust your food choices to balance yin or yang symptoms......

For a throbbing sinus headache (YIN), try miso soup with root vegetables. Visualize swollen capillaries contracting.

By contrast, for a tension headache and stiff neck (YANG), try a glass of apple juice or a fresh salad. Visualize tight muscles loosening and relaxing.

For Serious Symptoms, see a macrobiotic counselor and take cooking classes to more quickly understand which foods and cooking methods will help balance your condition. Read the rest of this book, and ask friends and family members to help you cook. You deserve special, loving attention!

Is the price of
these pleasures
more than we <u>all</u>
can afford?.....

Eat Local, Think Global.....

When you reach for a pleasure food, do you
often choose extremely expansive or contractive
foods imported from other climates?

Sugar, coffee, chocolate, tropical fruits.
Even the beef in your burger may come from
Mexico, Central or South America.

Historically, our passion for pleasure foods
dates back several hundred years. From
1500-1900, these foods fueled both the exotic
dreams and aggressive actions of Europeans
colonizing Africa and the New World. (For example,
sugar-cane production was responsible for an
appalling increase in the African slave trade in
the 1600's. See <u>Sugar Blues</u>, by William Dufty).

When entire societies become addicted to extreme
foods, the resulting social imbalances can be
dramatic and painful.....Right now, countless
people go hungry in Third World countries, while
their most fertile land is used to grow luxury
foods for industrialized nations (see <u>Diet for a
Small Planet</u>, and <u>Food First</u>, by Frances Moore
Lappe).

As world population swells, food-related issues
are becoming more urgent. Many modern farm
practices threaten the balance of natural forces
throughout the ecosphere.

For example, the market for fast-food burgers
is leading multi-national corporations to cut
down tropical rain forests at an alarming rate,
to grow grain for cattle. Rain forests supply a
major portion of the oxygen on earth. 1/2 the
life species on the planet live in these forests.

Our mutual survival is at risk.

IT'S BECOMING IMPOSSIBLE TO HEAL PERSONAL SYMPTOMS,
UNLESS THEY ARE UNDERSTOOD IN RELATIONSHIP TO THE NEED
TO HEAL THE PLANET.....

Your food choices make a difference.

Start with what you <u>don't</u> buy at the market
this week. You can pioneer a more simple,
globally responsible lifestyle, which
conserves natural resources, and helps
combat world hunger. One step at a time.

Eat local, think global.

Easily the most practical next step in a
new direction is to eat more locally-grown
whole foods. Shop around. In health food
stores, natural food co-ops, farmer's
markets. Look for organic fruits and
vegetables grown in your hometown or state.
Grains and beans grown in the USA. Sea
vegetables and medicinal herb teas harvested
in a temperate latitude. You'll be investing
in our mutual future.

Eat local, and think global, friends.
Together, we can make a big difference
towards creating the new lifestyle we're all
hungry for....ecological balance, economic
stability, emotional fulfillment, world
health and peace.

LOCAL PLEASURE

in a northern,
temperate climate....

apples
berries
strawberries
watermelon
canteloupe
honeydew
peaches
apricots
plums
pears
cherries
persimmons
grapes
raisins
other dried fruits
sunflower seeds
pumpkin seeds
almonds
walnuts
hazelnuts

Planetary Citizens Balance Sheet

HEALTHY CONTRACTION	HEALTHY EXPANSION
easy to focus, concentrate	relaxed, open-minded
assertive, determined	gentle, patient
rational, businesslike	creative, intuitive
independent	cooperative
can ask for what you need	sensitive, sympathetic

Can you tell which direction you need to move?
The following chart can help you choose the
right foods to reach your goal.....

How to Minimize High-Stress Foods

Feel tense, low energy, moody, or susceptible to illness?
You may want to avoid several high-stress foods
(listed in capitals below).

High-stress YANG foods are capitalized.
Stressful YIN foods are in caps, underlined.

Within each food group, foods are listed from the most
yang (contractive) to yin (expansive). Carrots, for
example, are quite a yang vegetable, potatoes very yin.
(Refer to the Balance Chart, p. 33, to understand why
carrots are a low-stress food, but potatoes may be
stressful--especially for people addicted to sweets or
alcohol).

✓ Check high-stress foods you especially want to avoid.

Animal Foods	Sweeteners	Oils
EGGS	amasake	sesame
RED MEAT	apple juice	safflower
POULTRY	brown rice syrup	corn
PORK	barley malt syrup	peanut
shrimp	maple syrup	olive
tuna	HONEY	PALM
salmon	FRUCTOSE	COCONUT
red snapper	MOLASSES	
sole	SUGAR	
halibut	ARTIFICIAL SWEETENERS	Seeds & Nuts
carp		
clam		sesame
oyster	Beverages	sunflower
		pumpkin
Dairy	twig tea (kukicha)	chestnut
	roasted barley tea	almond
GOAT CHEESE	grain coffee	walnut
HARD CHEESES	spring water	peanut
goat milk	non-aromatic herbs	CASHEW
soft cheese	aromatic herbs	MACADAMIA
low-fat milk	apple juice	
MILK	TROPICAL JUICES	
BUTTER	BLACK TEA	
SOUR CREAM	COFFEE	(continued)
YOGURT	ALCOHOL	
FROZEN YOGURT	ARTIFICIAL SODAS	
ICE CREAM		

Vegetables

burdock
carrot
watercress
winter squashes
parsley
parsnip
rutabega
onion
leek
green onion
turnip
radish
daikon
kale
collards
cabbage
chinese cabbage
romaine lettuce
broccoli
cauliflower
bok choy
beet
celery
crookneck squash
green beans
soft lettuces
chard
sweet peas
mushrooms
zucchini
sprouts
artichoke
asparagus
spinach
cucumber
GREEN PEPPER
POTATO
SWEET POTATO
YAM
TOMATO
EGGPLANT

Grains

buckwheat
millet
brown rice
wheat
rye
barley
oats
corn

Beans

aduki
garbanzo
lentil
black
kidney
pinto
lima
split pea
soybean
tempeh
tofu

Fruits

apple
strawberry
cherry
watermelon
apricot
pear
peach
lemon
raisin
prunes
oranges
grapes
BANANA
MANGO
AVOCADO
PAPAYA
DATES
PINEAPPLE
COCONUT
FIG

Sea Vegetables

hijiki
arame
sea palm
kombu
wakame
nori
agar agar

Herbs, Spices & Flavorings

garlic
parsley
thyme
oregano
basil
dill
cinnamon
CAROB
CHOCOLATE
CAYENNE (CHILI)
CHEMICAL FLAVORINGS
& PRESERVATIVES

Condiments

REFINED SALT
SEA SALT*
MISO*
TAMARI* (soy sauce)
grated ginger
fresh herbs
brown rice vinegar
CIDER VINEGAR
MUSTARD
MAYONNAISE
KETCHUP
HOT SAUCE

[* In excess, any salty condiment is stressful. However, in small quantities, sea salt, miso and tamari may be beneficial for your health. See the next page, to clarify your salt needs.]

✔ Now, go back with a colored pencil and check new, low-stress foods you'd like to try.

Deciding About Salt

Salt, the most contractive food, is essential for human survival.

We evolved from the sea, and our body fluids are in a saline solution. Salt maintains this solution and regulates the body's electrolytic balance. But we only need small amounts.

Salt needs vary with our changing life cycles. For example, babies, whose compact bodies grow and expand very quickly, need very little if any contractive salt. But mid-life adults often need a little salt daily to help maintain stamina and mental focus. Women with Pre-Menstrual Syndrome, however, often report that symptoms of bloating, irritability and sweet cravings can be relieved by reducing salt-intake 2 weeks before menstruation (the contractive phase of the menstrual cycle). Seniors, winding down from active careers, often find a low-salt diet helps them relax and appreciate life's subtle pleasures.

When buying salt, be aware that quality varies widely. Look for moist, hand-harvested sea salt, which contains many trace minerals (magnesium, zinc, copper, iodine, etc.). Refined salt, by contrast, has no trace minerals and often has sugar (dextrose) added.

NO SALT	BABIES seldom need salt. FOLKS RECOVERING from a diet high in salt, meat, cheese, eggs, and processed foods may need very little salt for 2-3 years.
A PINCH	GROWING CHILDREN, SENIOR CITIZENS, WOMEN after menopause, and women with Pre-Menstrual Syndrome need to be cautious... a little salt, but not too much.
LIGHTLY SALTY	TEENAGERS & MID-LIFE ADULTS often need lightly salty meals to maintain stamina and mental focus.
STRONG SALTY	PEOPLE RECOVERING from too much sugar, alcohol, caffeine, drugs (or even fruit juice and raw salad) may need to eat foods cooked with quite a salty taste for awhile, to help regain balance.

Tamari, miso, sauerkraut, pickles, umeboshi plums,
and tekka and shiso condiments are also good sources
of quality salt. But be careful. Salt is easy to
overdo. (As a general rule, I always serve
something unsalted in a meal.) Ask your body to
tell you if you need to cut down or add salt,
as follows:

CUT DOWN ON SALT IF YOU:	ADD A LITTLE SALT IF YOU:
feel too tense	can't focus
grind your teeth	feel run down
get too thirsty	get cold easily
crave sweets suddenly	feel overly sympathetic
feel tightness in your jaw	overeat sweets constantly

Outwitting Sugar

If you try to simply cut sugar out of your diet,
you're in for a great challenge.

Sugar is sneaky, seductive,
sentimental, and passionate.
And sugar is everywhere. That's expansive!

Go ahead. Try to throw it out.
Your guests will waltz in the door with a sugar dessert.
The kids will come home with it in their pockets.
The grandparents will beg you to be reasonable.

For your sanity's sake, fight back with alternatives!
Bake cookies in a rush of enthusiasm, using
apple juice, rice syrup or barley malt to sweeten 'em.

For a mellower sweet, try Almond Amasake Pudding,
or a homemade Sweet Squash Pie.

But for the most subtle sweetener of all....
Wait. Wait to taste, until the saliva rolls sweetly
on your tongue. Heavenly dew, the Japanese call it.
This sweetness is you.

(For fantastic Low-Guilt Dessert recipes, turn to Chapter 8).

Letting Go of Fat

From the firm, greasy fats in meat, eggs, and cheese....to munchable fats in nuts and seeds....to creamy, oily fats in butter, mayo, and salad dressing, fat is downright hard to resist. (Don't forget the sugary fats in ice cream, candy and cheesecake!)

40-45% of the Standard American Diet is fat. Growing scientific evidence links fat with heart disease, diabetes, and cancer. And many doctors now recommend that we cut our fat intake at least in half.

What Fat Does

* slows down blood-flow to the brain

* impairs function of liver, intestines, kidneys, lungs

* triggers hormone imbalance that can lead to PMS and reproductive cancers

* increases risk of allergies, diverticulitis, high blood pressure and many other degenerative conditions

---

If you want to let go of fat, however, it may be important to consider one fact most doctors don't discuss. Fat has a purpose. A positive reason for hanging around, helping to make your life work.

Think about the positive value of fat in <u>your</u> life, then try doing what I did. Say thanks.

"Thanks, fat, for the comfort. For insulating me from the jarring vibes of 20th century living. For slowing me down, when I get compulsive. And putting me to sleep, when I'm dog-tired.....

Thanks, especially, fat, for lip-smacking contentment, in a nuclear age of uncertainty.

I'll never forget your buttery pleasures. But now that I'm learning how to live more lightly on the Earth, and enjoy the benefits.....I'll pass."

The Big Fat Question:

Every food has a purpose in the great scheme of life. Can you guess the purpose of these?

Where's the Fat?

HIGH-STRESS FATS	LOWER-STRESS FATS	LOW-FAT

eggs
meat
fried foods
cheese
salmon
cream
whole milk
whole milk yogurt
butter
margarine
salad dressings
sour cream
cream cheese
mayonnaise
nuts
nut butters
palm oil
coconut oil
avocado
chips
candy bars
cookies & cakes
donuts
pizza
ice cream
	tofu
	tempeh
	pinto, lima, and chili beans
	soybeans
	poultry (without skin
	fish (white-meat)
	oatmeal
	soymilk products
	low-fat milk
	goat's milk products
	tofu spreads & dressings
	tahini (sesame butter)
	unrefined oils
	(small amounts)
	  sesame oil
	  olive oil
	  corn oil
	  sunflower oil
	sesame sunflower &
	  pumpkin seeds
	whole wheat tortillas
	granola (low-oil, no sugar)
	homemade cookies (low oil)
	pies with low-oil crust
	frozen yogurt
	Rice Dream
		whole grains
		whole grain pasta
		whole grain bread (no oil)
		aduki beans & lentils
		salads
		cooked vegetables
		wheatmeat (also "seitan")
		non-fat milk & yogurt
		creamy no-dairy soups
		(made w/grains & veggies)
		sea vegetables
		oil-free salad dressing
		kuzu and arrowroot
		  (for sauces & gravies)
		whole wheat bagels
		corn tortillas
		mochi (a chewy snack)
		rice cakes
		baked rice crackers
		homemade carrot butter
		amasake (rice nectar)
		fruit

HIGH-STRESS FATS: saturated animal fats, tropical oils & nuts, hydrogenated oils, and all foods that combine fat with white flour, sugar, or chemicals

LOW-STRESS FATS: unsaturated vegetable oil, beans, seeds, skimmed dairy, and treats made with natural, whole foods

LOW-FAT: most grains, vegetables, sea vegetables, fruit, and natural condiments

FAT TIP: Cut down on salt, if you want to cut down on fat. High-salt diets can create fat cravings.

FAT-DISSOLVING VEGGIES: radish
daikon radish
turnip
onion
green onion
leek
shiitake mushrooms

Principle #3: Use Food to Create Desired Effects

Most people are unaware of the fact that the kind of food they eat has a direct impact on their ability to accomplish their goals.

You brought special gifts here to Earth. Unknowingly, you may have been eating foods all your life that have held you back from fully using those talents.

Have you secretly longed to be an artist, a mountain climber, or an aggressive lawyer? Here's how you can start using food, to nourish your dream:

IF YOU FEEL:	BUT WANT TO FEEL:	Eat:
 Boxed into ruts, tense, overheated, overworked	 More creative, intuitive, sensitive, mellow & relaxed	LESS: salt meat eggs cheese hard, baked foods MORE: Gently Expansive Foods (see next page)
 Confused? Fatigued, spacy, moody, crave sweets, susceptible to everything	 More focused, assertive, physically active, & down-to-earth	LESS: sugar & honey raw food & juice ice cold food & drink potato & tomato alcohol, drugs, & food preservatives MORE: Mildly Contractive Foods (see p. 46)

Balancing Over-Contraction

A diet that includes lots of cheese, eggs, meat, tuna, salty chips and crackers, or even too many rice cakes can make you feel...

Heavy, slowed down, dry and thirsty, heated up, tense, sluggish or constipated, frustrated, irritable, or too intense about life.

To feel more relaxed, refreshed, inspired and creative, mellow, receptive and sensitive (yet still productive...), seek balance with:

Gently Expansive Foods

> assorted steamed veggies
> salad
> fresh corn or corn tortillas
> pot-boiled grains & beans
> whole grain pasta & breads
> tofu, tempeh, occasional fish
> local fruits & occasional juices
> sesame & sunflower seed condiments
> Low-Guilt Desserts (see Ch. 8)

To break the eggs-for-breakfast or cheese and chips habit, try these:

Balancing Recipes

Overnight Oats, P. 22
Morning Rice 'N Raisins, p. 98
Sesame Rice Balls, p. 160
Tofu Scramble, p. 103
Marinated Tempeh Cutlets, p. 103
Sunflower Rice Salad, p. 100
Crispy Cabbage Dill Salad, p. 68
Noodle Salad, p. 100
Chinese Vegetables DeLuxe, p. 100
Corn Polenta, p. 24

Burritos For Everybody, p. 107
Tofu Mayonnaise, p. 102
Millet Mashed Potatoes, p. 100
Lentil or Split Pea Soup, p. 77
Corn Chowder, p. 74
Fish Soup, p. 104
Bulghar Wheat Pilaf, p. 23
Steamed Greens, p. 68
Almond Crunch Pudding, p. 112
Mellow Jello, p. 113

Balancing Over-Expansion

A diet high in sugar, honey, coffee, milk, alcohol, drugs, and food additives....or even too much fruit, yoghurt, salad, potato, tomato, and hot sauce can lead to....

Constant sweet cravings, energy bursts followed by fatigue, cold hands and feet, no will power, feeling moody, dreamy, spaced out or confused, irregular bowels, recurring colds and infections.

To feel warm and energized, more assertive, clear and focused, fewer mood swings, calm steady energy, more regular bowels, and greater resistance to infection, seek balance with:

Mildly Contractive Foods

> pressure-cooked grains & beans
> roots & winter squashes
> sturdy dark greens
> buckwheat noodles
> miso soup
> sea vegetables, fish
> unyeasted sourdough breads
> the mildest desserts (see Ch. 8)
> toasted seed & sea vegetable condiments

Balancing Recipes

Miso Soup, p. 25
Pressure-Cooked Brown Rice, p. 20
Millet, p. 21
Sesame Salt, p. 24
Sea Palm Sunflower Crunch, p. 127
Aduki Squash Soup, p. 76
Black Bean Soup, p. 76
Ginger Baked Fish, p. 106
Chinese Vegetables DeLuxe, p. 105
Steamed Sturdy Greens, p. 70

One Pot Lentil Dinner, p. 128
Buckwheat or Millet Burgers, p. 164
Buckwheat Noodle Soup, p. 104
Millet Porridge, p. 98
Rich's Sesame Smother, p. 72
Cinnamon Squash, p. 70
Carrot Butter, p. 110
Soothy Applesauce, p. 112
Oatmeal-Raisin Cookies, p. 150
Creamy Rice Pudding, p. 148

The Breakfast Experiment

Here's an easy experiment that can reveal
the widely differing effects each food has on
your well-being.

For 5 days, eat just one food (as much as you
want of that food), each morning for breakfast.
Eat a different food each day. For example:

THE ONE FOOD EXPERIMENT

Day 1: fresh, local fruit or steamed veggies
Day 2: oatmeal or toast (no milk or butter)
Day 3: eggs, bacon, cheese, or sunflower seeds
Day 4: coffee, orange juice, or milk
Day 5: brown rice or millet

Sit quietly after you eat, and reflect. Note
how your energy level, moods, and physical
symptoms respond to this food throughout the
morning. Then, record your observations in a
journal, as follows:

SAMPLE FOOD JOURNAL:

	What I ate:	How I feel right after eating:	2 hours later:
Day 1:			

You may discover from this test that you are
unusually sensitive to certain foods. This
sensitivity or food allergy may be your body's way
of telling you to start cooking foods more appropriate
for your current life goals. Avoid irritating foods
for 1-3 months. Experiment with several new foods
(and/or maybe new life goals!)....Then, re-test
yourself for sensitivity.

All About Dairy

There's something terrifically appealing about milk.

Despite the fact that cow's milk is basically indigestable to humans, traditional peoples throughout Northern Europe, India, and parts of Northern Africa found that by boiling milk, or fermenting it into yoghurt and cheese, they could turn it into a highly pleasurable food that enriched life.

For centuries, it was enjoyed in small quantities as an addition to a grain-based diet. But in 20th century America, we have carried this experiment to an extreme....making milk, cheese, butter, and ice cream a large part of our staple diet.

According to many allergy specialists, behavior researchers, natural healers, and medical doctors, we may have gone too far. Consuming large quantities of dairy has had many negative effects on our health.

I encourage you to reflect on their findings, take time to experiment, and decide for yourself how dairy foods may be affecting your health:

* <u>Digestive disorders</u> often settle down when dairy is reduced. This is because casein, the major protein in milk, forms indigestable sticky curds in the stomach, which then line the intestinal walls and interfere with the ability to absorb nutrients (<u>Fit for Life</u>, Harvey & Marilyn Diamond).

* <u>Pre-Menstrual symptoms</u> such as bloating, headaches, irritability, confusion and cramps, often improve significantly on a dairy-free diet (<u>The Pre-Menstrual Syndrome Self-Help Book</u>, Susan Lark, M.D.).

* <u>Allergies</u> of all kinds are often benefited by non-dairy diets....chronic sinus conditions, food allergies, and environmental allergies. This may be because the by-products of milk

digestion create large quantities of mucus, which lead to sluggish organ function, lethargy and fatigue.

* Hyperactive or chronically fatigued kids are quite often allergic to dairy (as well as sugar and corn) according to William Crook, M.D., who has worked with thousands of allergic children (Don't Drink Your Milk, Frank Oski, M.D.).

* Breast cancer incidence is much higher in countries which consume lots of dairy foods. The high-fat content in diary can cause hormonal changes (by encouraging over-growth of estrogen-producing bacteria in the intestine). This estrogen imbalance is linked not only to breast cancer, but also to early onset of menstruation in puberty, heavy bleeding during menstruation, and late menopause (McDougall's Medicine, John McDougall, M.D.).

Experiment with a two-week trial dairy-free diet to discover if dairy is a factor in your current health problems. You may experience increased energy, weight loss, and more mental clarity. Sinus conditions may improve, but don't be surprised if you experience more discharge of mucus. Your body may be signalling you that it's glad to have a chance to get rid of dairy-caused mucus build-up.

To cut down on dairy gradually, try eliminating commercial whole milk products and substituting smaller quantities of low-fat raw milk, cheese, or yoghurt. These are less likely to contain harmful antibiotics and penicillin routinely used in large commercial dairies. Or, try goat's milk products. Lower in fat, these are more digestable to many people.

To increase non-dairy sources of calcium in your diet, eat at least one serving a day of dark leafy greens (see pp. 68-70). For even more concentrated calcium, include sea vegetables often (see p. 117).

For your convenience, in learning to cook more recipes without dairy, all the recipes in this book are dairy-free.

For Calcium:

Increase daily servings of dark leafy greens, such as kale, collards, watercress, turnip greens, and parsley.

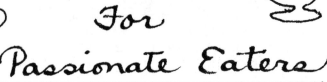

For Passionate Eaters

You're blessed.

God granted you the pleasure of loving
all flavors, textures, colors, aromas and sensations
that pass through your lips.

But if this chapter is making it clear that you need,
for your health's sake, to break free from rich, buttery,
creamy, spicy, sugary and salty foods, and ease into
some exotic alternatives, I'd suggest you start
with these:

CROWD PLEASERS	SWEET-TOOTH APPEASERS
Rice Wedding Salad	Aduki Squash Soup
Tofu Pizza & Lasagna	Cinnamon Squash
Marinara Spaghetti	Winter Simmer
Savory Stuffing & Brown Gravy	Sauteed Carrot Strengthener
Hummus	Baked Sweet Vegetables
Ginger Chicken Deluxe	Carrot Butter (try it on waffles!)
Tofu Scramble, Tofu Mayonnaise	Soothy Applesauce
Burritos for Everybody	Sweet Squash Pie
Noodle Salad w/ Sesame Dressing	Oatmeal Raisin Cookies
Ginger Baked Fish	Creamy Rice Pudding
Black Bean Soup	Strawberry Couscous Cake
Chinese Vegetables DeLuxe	Nana's Apple Cake
Sesame Waffles	Almond Crunch Pudding

Your homework....let us share your passion. Please
slurp, moan, and murmur your satisfaction (practice
with friends!). Slow down and savor. Tell the cook
(especially if it's you) how much you love the cooking
....morsel by morsel. It's OK to love this food--
it loves you, too!

The Food Combining Chart

Finally, it's important to know--especially if you have
sensitive digestion or food allergies--that how you
combine foods in a meal can make a big difference in
their digestibility:

Use this chart to help you plan the most harmonious meals:

EASY TO DIGEST   MOST GAS-FORMING

Grain with Vegetables   Fruit or Sweets with Beans

Pasta with Vegetables   Fruit with Vegetables

Beans with Vegetables   Fruit with grain, dairy or meat

Fish with Vegetables   Grain with dairy or meat

Cooked local fruit (alone)   Melons with anything else

Melons (alone)

IN SUMMARY

Whether you're a moody artist or robust construction
worker....whether you have a passion for food
or bothersome food allergies....the Self-Healing
Principles in this chapter can help you tailor
your food choices to create new balance in
your body, your moods, and your life:

Principle #2:   BALANCE NATURE'S FORCES IN COOKING

Principle #3:   USE FOOD TO CREATE DESIRED EFFECTS

Beyond your personal healing, these principles
can also help you take positive steps towards
solving pressing planetary issues.

Remember to Eat Local, Think Global, friend.
You'll be helping to alter agricultural and
marketing practices that threaten our
mutual survival on Earth. It's enough to
make you go out and order a Low-Fat Special,
isn't it?

Cooking With Spark

It's on the edge of your knife.
It's at rest, in the core of your wooden spoon,
Waiting for you to stir.
It dances on the curly edges of the kale.
Then, bubbles in the pot.
And, it's in you.

The elusive spark that heals.

In oriental philosophy, this light and lively energy
has a name. They call it ki or chi. When we know
how to let it flow, it can fill us, vitalizing every cell....

It's the mysterious stuff of life. Watch for it
sparkling in the water. Season your cooking with
it daily. You may soon come alive with potency (potential
for an exciting, adventurous life). More than ever imagined.

But watch out. It is potent stuff. When this spark
touches and flows through areas of your life or your
body which have become stagnant or diseased, it
can shake up the old and quickly usher in the new
and unexpected.

Cook with spark, and you may find yourself in
bed. With a runny nose, a cough, or a mild fever.
Letting new energy into your body can prompt your
cells to clean out old, accumulated toxins,
making space for new, healthy cells to flourish.

If so, go with the flow. Imagine there's light
in your blood, gently shining into all the dark
places. Then, turn to the Healing Foods Glossary
(p. 195). You may find that some simple home
remedies from traditional oriental medicine
can help you get back on your feet more
quickly than usual.

What does it feel like when it settles down, this spark?
Energized, but calm. Watch for it everywhere.

3 Variety with Vegetables and Soups

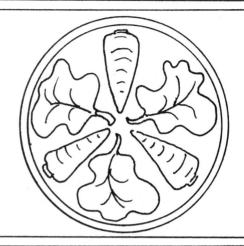

Ever had a daikon radish? Long, white and friendly-looking, it tastes hot and crispy when raw. But mellow, tender and even a little sweet when cooked. Also, it's well-known in the Orient for its ability to dissolve excess mucus and body fat. Getting curious to taste it?

This chapter can help you graduate from the standard American veggie sampler of peas, corn, potatoes, lettuce, green beans, and tomatoes.... and discover how to simmer-up over 45 varieties of the most strengthening and nutritious seasonal vegetables.

Try baked buttercup squash in autumn for savory-sweet comfort. Or steamed kale or turnip greens in spring for envigoration, Vitamin C, calcium, fiber and iron. Or, low-fat Cream of Broccoli Soup in any season, for a happy belly....

Shop for organic. Trust your instincts to find the liveliest.

As fresh flavors reach out to gently embrace your tastebuds, the memory of buttery, cheese-laden, overcooked, soggy, and frozen vegetables will gradually fade.

New pleasures await. Crispiness, crunch, and color. Melt-in-your mouth sweetness. And the satisfaction of finding specific veggies and soups that improve your moods and boost your energy levels.

If you grow to love 'em and suspect you'd also love to grow them, see p. 205 for a list of seed companies dedicated to renewing the Earth's life-giving greenery.

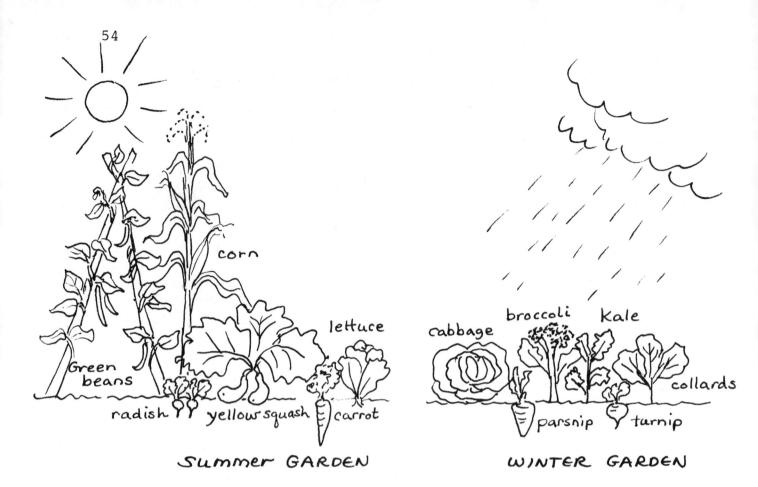

Summer GARDEN   WINTER GARDEN

Eating With The Seasons

Locally grown, seasonal vegetables help you adapt to your surroundings by subtly connecting you to the rhythm of the seasons. More contractive vegetables such as carrots, kale, collards, broccoli, parsnip, rutabaga, and turnip, will not only weather a frost, but taste sweeter afterwards. We gain stamina and vitality when we eat them in winter.

More expansive vegetables such as leaf lettuce, corn on the cob, green beans, cucumber, and summer squash, have a higher water content that enables them to thrive in the heat. We can stay cool by emphasizing these in our summer diet.

Many vegetables grow well in more than one season of the year. Talk to local gardeners, or read up in seed catalogues (see Selected Reading, p.205), to learn which ones are in season in your area. Traditional winter vegetables in very cold climates include pickles and dried vegetables in addition to the vegetables that do well in cold storage--onions, winter squashes, roots, and cabbages.

Look on the next page for a shopping guide to healing vegetables which thrive in a northern temperate climate.

The Most Beneficial Vegetables

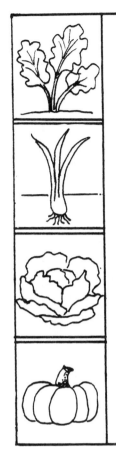

Dark Green & Leafy Green Vegetables

kale	bok choy	roquette
collards	chinese cabbage	kohlrabi
mustard greens	leaf lettuce	wild greens:
turnip tops	romaine lettuce	(dandelion,
watercress	parsley	chickweed, etc.)

The Fat-Dissolvers

radish	onion	shiitake
daikon radish	green onion	mushrooms
turnip	leek	

The Cabbage Family

all kinds of	broccoli	brussels sprouts
cabbage	cauliflower	(see below, too!)

Nutritions Roots & Winter Squash

carrot	Squashes:	hokkaido pumpkin
parsnip	acorn	hubbard
rutabaga	butternut	pumpkin
burdock	buttercup	sweet mama
lotus root	delicata	spaghetti squash

DARK LEAFY GREENS: At least one serving of these daily will enrich your diet with vital chlorophyll, iron, calcium, Vit. C, Vit. A, and intestinal cleansing fiber.

FAT-DISSOLVING VEGGIES: Need to lose weight or lower your blood cholesterol? Chinese medicine recommends eating radish, daikon, onion, green onion, leeks and shiitake mushrooms to dissolve fats and excess mucus.

THE CABBAGE FAMILY: Full of nutrients that help prevent cancer-- along with cabbages, this big family includes broccoli, cauliflower, kale, collards, bok choy, radish, turnip, daikon, kohlrabi, watercress, roquette, and mustard greens (study on Diet and Cancer, Nat'l Academy of Sciences, 1982).

ROOTS & WINTER SQUASH: Also cancer-preventing, these hearty veggies are great sources of Vit. A, beta-carotene, minerals and fiber.

To reduce sweet-
cravings, eat more
sweet vegetables.

Nightshade Veggies:

Tomato
Potato
Eggplant
Green Pepper
Red Pepper

High-Oxalic Veggies:

Chard
Spinach
Beets
Rhubarb

Have a Sweet-Tooth?

Cooked sweet vegetables can do wonders to calm a sweet-tooth and even out your physical energy and moods. Cook them in puddings, pies, soups, or stews.

By contrast, intense sweets such as sugar, honey, molasses or maple syrup may aggravate a sweet-tooth, and cause bursts of hyper energy followed by fatigue.

Too much fruit or fruit juice can cause these energy crashes, too (most fruits are higher in sugar than sweet veggies).

So, if you need calming snacks for kids... try winter squash, yams, parsnips, or carrots--steamed, baked or pureed into spreads or puddings. These are great for diabetics, too (see Carrot Butter, p. 110).

Nightshades and Other Stressful Vegetables

Nightshades (which include tomato, potato, eggplant and peppers) are one group of veggies you may want to minimize--especially in times of stress.

Studies show they speed the heart-rate and slow down digestion. They're high in alkaloids, which block B Vitamin absorption (key vitamins in coping with stress). And they may contribute to arthritic and rheumatic symptoms (see The Nightshades & Health, by Norman Childers).

Other veggies that are potentially stressful on the body include chard, spinach, beets, and rhubard. These contain oxalic acid, which binds calcium and eliminates it from the body--increasing the risk of osteoporosis and kidney stones.

All these yin vegetables are an appealing balance to extremely yang foods like meat, eggs, and cheese. But on a Self-Healing Diet, you may want to temporarily avoid them, while your body gains strength and learns a new, more gentle way to stay in balance. (For a great tomato-free spaghetti sauce, see p. 166).

Organic Does Make a Difference

Researchers at Rutgers University have shown that non-organic produce from the supermarket is lacking in trace minerals--with as little as 25% the mineral content of organic vegetables from health food stores. The following chart shows the results.

Organic foods taste better, and eating them frequently reduces the risk of ingesting and accumulating all the chemicals used in commercial food production. Growers use chemical fertilizers, soil fumigants, and pesticides. Distributors and stores use dyes and wax, dip and spray vegetables to retard spoilage. For example, celery is sometimes dipped in formaldehyde.

Organic vegetables, by contrast, are grown and handled by a network of people committed to developing a sustainable, ecological agriculture that promotes our health and restores fertility to the soil. The qualitative difference is well worth the difference in price.

VARIATIONS in MINERAL CONTENT in VEGETABLES. Firman E. Baer report, Rutgers Uni.

	Percentage of dry weight		Millequivilents per 100 grams dry weight				Trace Elements parts per million dry matter				
	Total Ash or Mineral Matter	Phosphorous	Calcium	Magnesium	Potassium	Sodium	Boron	Manganese	Iron	Copper	Cobalt
SNAP BEANS											
Organic	10.45	0.36	40.5	60.0	99.7	8.6	73	60	227	69.0	0.26
Inorganic	4.04	0.22	15.5	14.8	29.1	0.0	10	2	10	3.0	0.00
CABBAGE											
Organic	10.38	0.38	60.0	43.6	148.3	20.4	42	13	94	48.0	0.15
Inorganic	6.12	0.18	17.5	13.6	33.7	0.8	7	2	20	0.4	0.00
LETTUCE											
Organic	24.48	0.43	71.0	49.3	176.5	12.2	37	169	516	60.0	0.19
Inorganic	7.01	0.22	16.0	13.1	53.7	0.0	6	1	9	3.0	0.00

Choosing Vegetables for Your Moods

Most people can sense how very stimulating foods affect their moods. Coffee gives you alertness, followed by a letdown. Chocolate makes you feel loved, then mildly depressed and wanting more chocolate. Red meat fuels assertiveness, but also leads to lethargy.

Unlike these extreme foods, which tend to exaggerate moods, vegetables have very subtle effects on your moods and personality. Use them to shift your moods gently in the direction you want them to go.

FEEL TENSE, ANGRY OR STUCK?

Eat crisp, succulent veggies:

chinese cabbage or bok choy
green beans
romaine lettuce
cucumber or radish
cauliflower
celery
snap peas

These will help you relax, lighten up and feel clear. Have them either lightly cooked, or in salads.

FEEL SUPERSENSITIVE, OR TOO EMOTIONAL?

Eat more cooked veggies...especially roots, winter squash & sturdy greens:

daikon
carrot
turnip
butternut or buttercup squash
kale
collards

These can calm you and help you get down to business. Give you a firmer grip on life, and fuel productive creativity.

If you swing between these two extremes....choose appropriate veggies to balance your moods each day.

Choosing Cooking Methods For Your Health

Every cooking method can have a unique effect on your body, mind, and mood.

Common sense can help you find the ones that are best for your health in each season. All you need to do is ask yourself: "How do I want to feel?"

Check the weather, as well as your moods. For example, on a hot day in August (or anytime you want to cool down and relax), how could you fix carrots, to help you feel great? What about a glass of cool carrot juice, or a refreshing carrot salad?

Now, imagine a bitter cold day in January (or anytime when you want to feel warm, comforted, and strong). Would you enjoy carrot juice or salad as much? Would you feel satisfied, afterwards? Or, would you rather have carrots simmered in a soup, or baked in a pie?

The Carrot Experiment

The "Carrot Experiment" on the following page, is a simple but potent exercise I use in cooking class to help people sense the effects of different cooking methods. You may want to try it now, if you have the ingredients on hand.

You'll be preparing carrots in two very different ways. Before you start, ask yourself: "How do I want to feel? Lighter? Calmer? Warmed?" Then, notice the distinct physical sensations, thoughts, and feelings you experience as you taste each dish. Everything you notice will help you streamline your cooking methods to your own special needs.

The Carrot Experiment

Preparation:

Choose a time when you can relax and focus in the kitchen. Gather your ingredients as if you were a scientist preparing for an experiment, or an artist spreading out tools to create a work of art. Select special dishes to serve yourself. Then, stretch, breathe, and invite your senses to be especially open while you cook and taste.

STEP 1: Melt-in-Your Mouth Carrots

1 carrot
1 small parsnip or turnip
6" strip kombu
water
tamari soy sauce

Simmer in a small skillet with a lid....

Place kombu in 1/4" water in a small skillet. Let it soak and soften. Cut carrot in diagonal slices. Lay each slice flat, and cut into 3 or 4 lenghwise strips (see illustration above). Slice parsnip or turnip similarly. Place roots on top of kombu. Bring to a boil, cover, and simmer 25 minutes.

(While this simmers, prepare the salad in Step 2).

When done, the water should be mostly absorbed. Remove kombu (or, if you prefer, slice it attractively and add to the dish). Serve yourself a small, elegant portion and sit down to enjoy Step 3.

STEP 2: Sweet Carrot Salad

The finer you grate a carrot, the sweeter it tastes....

1 small carrot
a big leaf of romaine lettuce
sqeeze of lemon
dash of dill

Finely shred the lettuce with a knife. Arrange on a pretty plate. Grate carrot finely and mound on top of lettuce. Add a squeeze of lemon, and a dash of dill.

Let it sit a few minutes while you complete Step 1, then go on to Sensuous Tasting....

STEP 3: Sensual Tasting

Before you taste....

Pause to smell. Take in the beauty of each dish. Breathe!

Take a bite. Let the flavors greet your tongue. Feel your mouth water. Then, chew. Close your eyes. Picture a landscape where this food would taste best to you. Describe or draw that scene.

Repeat these sensuous eating techniques with the second dish. Look, smell, and let your mouth water. Chew. Imagine an environment that most suits this food.

Then, turn the page to evaluate what you've learned, in Step 4.

STEP 4: Evaluation

1] Review your experience. Which carrot dish felt most balancing for you? Talk to a friend about what you noticed (or, write a poem in your journal about each dish!).

2] What were the most important factors in making one of these foods feel more right for you? (Number from 1-9, most to least important).

   ____ how you cut it   ____ your mood

   ____ foods you put with   ____ today's weather
        the carrot

                     ____ artful serving

   ____ cooking method   ____ visualization
        (slow-simmer vs. raw)

   ____ sensuous tasting   ____ other

3] Which dish was more expansive? (Guess, then look below).

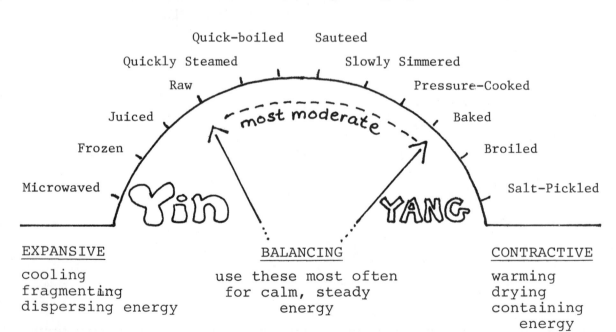

COOKING METHODS

Quick-boiled   Sauteed

Quickly Steamed   Slowly Simmered

Raw   Pressure-Cooked

most moderate

Juiced   Baked

Frozen   Broiled

Microwaved   Salt-Pickled

Yin   **YANG**

EXPANSIVE	BALANCING	CONTRACTIVE
cooling	use these most often	warming
fragmenting	for calm, steady	drying
dispersing energy	energy	containing energy

SUMMER + WINTER STYLE COOKING

Summer Style (YIN)

In warm weather, use more expansive cooking methods, to help you lighten up and relax:

- Steam, quick-boil, or make salads

- Serve cool or room temperature

- Eat lighter--more upward-growing foods

- Choose soft, leafy greens

- Use less salt

- Enhance with vinegar, lemon, fresh ginger, parsley, or other fresh herbs

Winter Style (YANG)

In cool weather, use more contractive methods, for comfort, warmth and strength.

- Slow-simmer, pressure-cook, bake, or saute

- Serve warm

- Eat hearty--more compact veggies & downward growing roots

- Choose sturdy, leafy greens

- Add a little sea salt, miso, tamari or sauerkraut

- Enhance with green onion, sea vegetables, ginger, or dried herbs

64

A Taste For Health

If you continue to experiment with carrots
and other vegetables in this same spirit, you
can learn fairly quickly how to sense the
healing qualities of specific vegetables and
cooking methods.

As this happens, you'll need to rely less and
less on outside information to tell you what
your body needs. Eventually, you may know
even before you put a food in your mouth, how
it's going to make you feel.

You'll be able to sense whether you need more
raw food or more cooked food, more light, refreshing, expansive meals, or more hearty, warming,
contractive meals, to stay in balance physically
and emotionally. This "taste for health" is
the most essential ingredient in a self-healing
diet.

SUMMARY

Need a pizza, ice cream, or burger, to balance
all this new sensitivity? Go ahead!

Simply trust that the information in this
chapter is tucked away safely inside you, ready
to sprout like green seedlings whenever you
shine the light.

Just think of lively, organic, locally grown
vegetables, in season. Dark greens, roots, and
winter squash are the most beneficial. Potato
and tomato may be stressful if you're under stress.
Different cooking methods work best in each
season....

Let it all grow on you naturally, while you try
some of my favorite recipes for savory vegetable
side dishes and soups.

Recipes:

VEGETABLES & SOUPS

VEGETABLE COOKING METHODS

WARM WEATHER VEGETABLES

Steamed Leafy Greens
Colorful Shredded Veggies
Crookneck Saute
Quick-Boiled Salad
Tangy Cabbage

COOL WEATHER VEGETABLES

Steamed Sturdy Greens
Winter Simmer
Cinnamon Squash
Sweet Baked Vegetables
Sauteed Carrot Strengthener

FRIENDLY INVENTIONS

Rich's Sesame Smother

SOUPS

Soup Stock
The Easiest Vegetable Soup

CREAMY GRAIN SOUPS

Cream of Broccoli
Summer Corn Chowder
Christmas Parsnip Soup
Barley Mushroom Soup
Sunny Buckwheat Soup

HEARTY BEAN SOUPS

Black Bean Soup
Aduki-Squash Soup
Lentil Soup with Noodles
Split Pea Miso

Vegetable Cooking Methods

To steam fresh vegetables at the same time that you reheat leftover rice, a stainless steel steamer comes in handy (look for the kind that sets on top of a saucepan).

For savory baked vegetable combinations, an enameled cast-iron pot works well. Also, this can double as a stovetop stew pot.

STEAM

Almost every vegetable tastes delicious simply steamed until tender. Whenever you are curious to taste a new vegetable, try this first. Greens take 5 to 10 minutes. Roots and squashes 15-25 minutes, depending on how thickly you slice them.

WATER-SAUTÉ

Roots and greens taste great together, with this method. Place 1/2" water in a skillet and bring to a boil. Add thin-sliced roots, cover and simmer 5-8 minutes, just until tender. Then, add greens and simmer just a few minutes so they stay bright green--a beautiful contrast with the roots. The water will be almost gone, the flavor and texture delectable.

BAKE

Winter squashes and roots get very sweet when you bake them. Especially if you cook them in a covered pot, together with a strip of kombu or wakame seaweed. Put 1/4" water in the pot, add vegetables and bring to a boil on the stovetop first. Sprinkle with tamari, cover & bake at 375° for 1 hour. Mix and match:

rutabaga   jerusalem artichoke
leek   winter squash
onion   turnip
daikon   parsnip
carrot   celery root

OIL-SAUTÉ

For rich-flavored vegetables, rub your favorite skillet with toasted sesame oil (a few drops to 1 tsp. for 2 c. veggies). Add sliced vegetables and stir over medium heat for a few minutes. Add 1/4" water, cover and simmer 8-10 minutes, until water is nearly gone and the vegetables are nice and tender. Season with a sprinkle of tamari. For bright color, garnish with thin-sliced green onion.

An old-fashioned cast-iron (or enameled) skillet gives sauteed veggies a rich, mellow flavor.

DO YOU HAVE A GOOD KNIFE?

A sharp, well-balanced knife should glide through a carrot as easy as your foot slides into a sheepskin slipper. What pleasure!

Look for Caddie, Mac, or a good quality Japanese vegetable knife (see illustration). Stainless won't rust, but a carbon-edged knife stays sharp longer. The 11" size is most versatile.

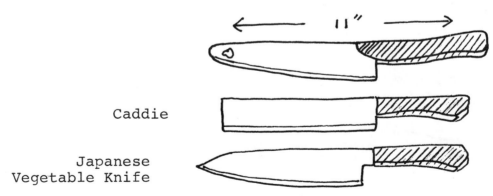

Caddie

Japanese
Vegetable Knife

Warm Weather Vegetables

Steamed Leafy Greens

Bok Choy
Chinese Cabbage
Mustard Greens
Radish Greens
Turnip Greens
Watercress

A daily helping of one of these
greens, lightly steamed (3-5 minutes)
will give you a rich supply of vitamins and minerals, fiber, and most
of all....aliveness! (The first
2 are also delicious raw in salads).

Colorful Shredded Veggies

1 tsp. finely grated ginger
1 c. fine-chopped broccoli
1 small carrot, grated
handful of fresh peas
3-4 finely shredded cabbage
or chinese cabbage leaves
1 green onion, sliced
1/4 - 1/3 c. water

Sensuous and crunchy--the secret is
cooking these quickly! In a skillet,
boil water, add broccoli stems, carrot,
peas & ginger. Cover & simmer 3 minutes. Then add broccoli tops, cabbage,
and green onion. Cook just until they
wilt (about 1 minute). Serve as a
side dish, or rolled in a whole wheat
chapati with Tofu Mayo (see p. 165).

Crookneck Sauté

1 onion, sliced thinly
2 yellow crookneck squash
1/2 bunch watercress
or, 2 kale leaves

Artfully cut, this yellow and green
sidedish is a beauty. Slice squash
on the diagonal. Cut stems of watercress finely, and leaves in larger
pieces. Or, cut kale along the lines
of growth, and chop stems finely.
To water-saute, boil 1/4" water, add
onion and squash, cover, and
simmer 5 minutes. Then, add
greens and simmer 5 minutes
more (this keeps them green).

Quick-Boiled Salad

Choose from:

broccoli
cabbage
carrot
celery
chinese cabbage
daikon
green beans
green onion
parsley
radish
radish greens
snow peas
watercress

Popular in the Orient, this salad is refreshing and very digestable. Choose 3 to 5 vegetables. Cut them in attractive, small shapes. Boil 1 quart water and cook each vegetable separately until it's just crunchy (2-3 minutes). Dip out with a slotted spoon and cool in a large strainer. (Save the cooking liquid--its great for soups or sauces). Toss veggies in a bowl and sprinkle with lemon juice or rice vinegar, and a dash of tamari.

FOR MORE SALADS & SALAD DRESSING,

See pp. 100-101

Tangy Cabbage

1 c. green cabbage
1 slivered onion
1 ear fresh corn (optional)
1 umeboshi plum*

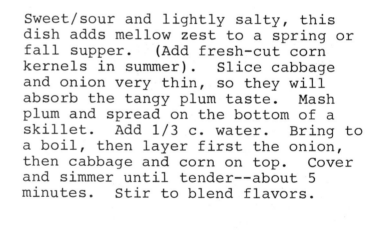

Sweet/sour and lightly salty, this dish adds mellow zest to a spring or fall supper. (Add fresh-cut corn kernels in summer). Slice cabbage and onion very thin, so they will absorb the tangy plum taste. Mash plum and spread on the bottom of a skillet. Add 1/3 c. water. Bring to a boil, then layer first the onion, then cabbage and corn on top. Cover and simmer until tender--about 5 minutes. Stir to blend flavors.

*Umeboshi is a salt-pickled plum used often in Oriental cooking. Very alkaline, it aids digestion. It's tangy sour flavor also helps to detoxify the liver (which gets stressed on a diet high in fats). See Healing Foods Glossary, p. 203.

Cool Weather Vegetables

Steamed Sturdy Greens

collards
daikon greens
kale
kohlrabi greens
savoy or green cabbage
turnip greens

Have a daily serving of one of these sturdy greens, for an abundant supply of Vitamin C, beta carotene, iron, calcium and other essential nutrients. Steam 5-10 minutes, until tender.

Winter Simmer

4 c. butternut, buttercup, or banana squash
2 stalks celery
6" strip wakame seaweed
1 onion, cut in 8
3/4 c. water
tamari soy sauce

Cut open the squash and scoop out the seeds. Lay flat surface on a cutting board and peel, by shaving with a sharp knife from top to bottom. Dice in 1" chunks. Bring water to a boil. Crumble or cut wakame in small pieces. Put everything in the pot. Boil, then cover and simmer 20-30 minutes, until squash is tender. Season to taste with tamari.

Cinnamon Squash

1 delicata or acorn squash (or, wedges or chunks of banana, butternut, buttercup, or hubbard squash)
cinnamon

Delicata tastes as good as it sounds... wonderfully delicate and sweet. Cut squash in half and scoop out seeds. Sprinkle liberally with cinnamon. Rub a covered baking pot with sesame oil. Place squash in pot with 1/4" water. Bring to boil on the stove-top, then cover and bake at 375-400° for 45 minutes, or until tender.

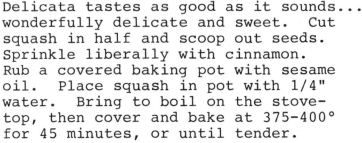

acorn

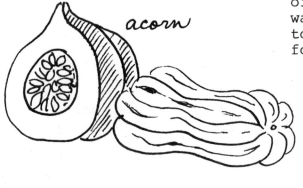

delicata

Sweet Baked Vegetables

carrots
leeks
parsnips
onion
jerusalem artichoke
rutabaga
wakame or kombu seaweed

Mix and match, in duets, trios, or quartets. The flavors of all these sweet vegetables blend very nicely. Rub a covered baking pot with toasted sesame oil. Cut vegetables in hearty chunks or slices. Place in pot with 1/4" water. Bring water to a boil on the stovetop, then cover and bake 45 minutes at 375°.

Sautéed Carrot Strengthener

1 carrot, cut julienne
1 c. burdock*, cut julienne
(or, if unavailable, use
parsnip or rutabaga)
¼ tsp. sesame oil
tamari soy sauce

This traditional Japanese side-dish (called "Kinpira") can warm you to the toes in cold weather, build your stamina by improving blood quality, and increase your mental clarity!

Slice the carrot and burdock in long, thin, diagonal slices. Cut each slice into matchsticks. Saute burdock lightly in an oiled skillet, stirring over medium heat. Add carrot, and 1/2" water. Boil, then cover and simmer 20 minutes. Check and add water, if needed, but let it get all absorbed at the end, for the best flavor. Sprinkle lightly with tamari, and stir. Serve small portions.

*Burdock - a long, brown-skinned root with savory flavor. Highly mineralized, and known in many herbal traditions for its blood-cleansing ability. Eating it often can also increase vitality. Find it in Oriental markets, or grow your own (for seeds, look on the Resources page, under Gardening, p. 205.

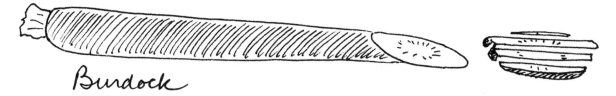

Burdock

Friendly Inventions

Steamed Veggie Mandala

Steam seasonal veggies just
until crunchy. Arrange
artfully on a bed of
leaf lettuce. Serve
with Tofu Mayo (p. 165)
or Lemon Vinaigrette
(p. 101).

It's easy to invent your own colorful
and tasty combination dishes with fresh
vegetables. Just start with two veggies
that sound good together to you, and
experiment. For example, how many of these
have you tried?

green beans and cauliflower
green beans and onion
green beans and fresh corn
green beans and green onions
green beans and parsley
green beans and celery
green beans and daikon radish
green beans and cucumber

Pick one that sounds especially inviting.
How would you cook it?

in soup
steamed
sauteed
in salad
baked in a casserole with noodles
fried with rice
slivered real thin
or cut in bite-size morsels.....

Here's one of my husband Rich's super
inventions, that's different in
season:

Baked "Sesame Smother"

This one goes over
big with company....

Rich's Sesame Smother

Steam two or three veggies. Put them
in a baking dish. Smother them with
Sesame Gravy (see p. 164). Top the
whole thing with sourdough breadcrumbs
and bake until it bubbles. This one
always tastes great!

Soups

Soup Stock

Homemade soup stock gives any soup a
special, rich flavor. Save the ends and
bits whenever you cut vegetables (outer
leaves of cabbage, tops of celery, parsley
stems, etc.). Keep them in a jar in the
fridge. When you have plenty, simmer them
up in a quart of water for 20-30 minutes.
Strain and refrigerate.

The Easiest Vegetable Soup

Surprisingly quick and tasty soups can
be made with just 2 or 3 vegetables, water,
stock, and a dash of tamari, miso, or herbs.

The trick? Boil the water or stock first, to
keep the veggies from getting soggy. Add the harder
vegetables (roots, winter squash, stems) and cook until
nearly soft. Then add the light ones (greens, celery,
cauliflower, broccoli tops). Simmer until just
crunchy or tender. Flavor to taste, and
garnish with parsley or green onion.
Here are some of my favorites....

Delicious Combinations:

Broccoli and onion
Buttercup squash, celery, and onion
Butternut squash, cabbage & onion
Daikon and daikon greens
Jerusalem artichokes & kale
Leeks and parsnips
Onion and shiitake mushrooms
Turnip & turnip greens
Yellow crookneck squash & green onion

Light, Creamy Soups

Cream of Broccoli

5 c. water or stock
1½ c. chopped broccoli
1 small onion, diced
1½ c. cooked brown rice
or, leftover oatmeal
barley or white miso

VARIATIONS:

mushroom & onion
leeks and carrot
cauliflower and green onion

Bring water or stock to a boil and add diced broccoli stems and onion. Cover and simmer 10 minutes. Put 2 c. of the soup liquid in the blender with rice or oatmeal. Blend until smooth, then return to the pot. Add broccoli tops and simmer until they're tender. Flavor with miso to taste.

Summer Corn Chowder

5 c. water or stock
kernals cut from 3 ears corn
1 onion, diced
1 stalk celery, diced
¼ c. daikon radish (optional)
3" strip kombu seaweed
barley miso, to taste
parsley

Simmer corn cobs and kombu in water for 10 minutes. Then remove cobs, add onion, celery, & daikon. Simmer 10 minutes, then add corn kernals and cook 10 minutes more. Dissolve miso into soup and remove kombu. For creamy texture, blend half in the blender. Reheat, and serve garnished with parsley.

Christmas Parsnip Soup

5 c. water
4 c. parsnips, cut in chunks
1 c. diced broccoli
a pinch of sea salt
or mellow miso, to taste

(thin with extra water, after blending, for desired consistency)

My favorite Christmas dinner soup...fragrant and elegant. Boil water and simmer parsnips 15 minutes or until tender. Blend smooth, then return to the pot and add broccoli. Simmer 15-20 minutes, until broccoli is soft, and the flavors have blended into a mellow union. Season with salt or miso, to taste.

Warming Grain Soups

Barley Mushroom Soup

1 onion, diced
2 cloves garlic, minced
¼ tsp. sesame oil
½ c. hulled barley
6 - 8 c. water
6" strip kombu
2 dried shiitake mushrooms
1 carrot, diced
1 stalk celery & leaves, diced
1 bay leaf
½ tsp. dill
1 c. cabbage, diced
2 T. barley or soybean miso

Variations:

Add fresh corn in summer,
burdock in winter,
watercress in spring or fall

Exquisitely creamy and tasty when
you make it a day ahead of time--
but if that's not possible, at
least soak the barley overnight.

Oil the soup pot and saute onion
and garlic for a few minutes.
Add water, barley, kombu and
shiitake. Bring to a boil and
simmer 45 minutes. Then, add carrot,
celery, bay leaf and dill. Simmer
30 minutes more, or until barley
is tender. Add cabbage and cook
15 minutes more. Turn off heat,
add miso, and serve garnished
with parsley.

Sunny Buckwheat Soup

1/3 c. buckwheat
2 c. chopped cabbage
2 c. diced butternut squash
or. banana squash
1 small onion, diced
1 strip wakame seaweed
4 c. water
½ tsp. sea salt
parsley to garnish

Buckwheat, which thrives in cold
climates, is very hearty and warming.
Try this sweet soup for breakfast,
or a surprisingly filling supper
on a cold day.

Roast the buckwheat, by stirring in
a skillet over medium heat until it
turns golden brown and smells toasty.
Bring the water to a boil with onion,
squash, and wakame (cut in small
pieces). Add buckwheat and cabbage.
Simmer 10 minutes, then add salt.
Serve garnished with fresh parsley.

Hearty Bean Soups

Black Bean Soup

1 c. black beans
4 c. water
6" strip kombu seaweed
2 C. chopped cauliflower
1 carrot, diced
1 tsp. finely grated ginger
pinch cumin (optional)
1 green onion, sliced
2-3 tsp. tamari soy sauce

Variation:

If available, include
2 collard leaves, sliced
(add with the cauliflower)

Wash and soak the black beans overnight. Drain soaking water and add
fresh. Place in the pressure cooker
with kombu, bring to pressure, and
simmer for 1 hour. (Or, pot boil for
2½ hours). Bring down from pressure,
add cauliflower, ginger, carrot and
cumin and simmer 20 minutes more--
just until veggies are tender. Stir
in the green onion, season with
tamari, and let it sit awhile before
serving, to let the flavors blend.
Garnish with slivers of fresh green
onion. Tastes even better the next
day.

Aduki Squash Soup

½ c. aduki beans
6" strip kombu seaweed
4 c. water
1 c. buttercup or
butternut squash, cubed
½ tsp. sea salt, or to taste
1 green onion, sliced

Sweet and hearty, this soup is
especially good for diabetics, or
anybody with strong sweet cravings.

Bring beans, kombu, and water to a
boil. Cover and simmer 1 hour. Peel
and cut squash, add and simmer ½ hour
more, or until squash is tender
enough to dissolve. Season with
sea salt and add green onion (save
a few slivers to garnish each bowl).

Butternut

Buttercup

Lentil Noodle Soup

1 c. lentils
6 c. water
1 strip wakame seaweed
  cut in ½" pieces
1 onion, diced
2 cloves garlic
1 carrot, sliced diagonal
1 parsnip, diced (optional)
1 c. diced kale or watercress
2/3 c. whole wheat noodles
3 T. barley miso

Layer lentils, wakame, onion, garlic, and root vegetables in a pot. Pour in water, bring to a boil, and simmer for 30 minutes. Add greens and noodles and simmer another 20 minutes. Dissolve miso into soup just before serving.

Kids love this one. Try whole wheat alphabet noodles, too.

Split Pea Miso

1 c. split peas
1 strip wakame or kombu
1 onion, diced
1 clove garlic
1/8 c. burdock, slivered
1 carrot or parsnip
1 stalk celery, diced
½ tsp. thyme and marjoram
2 T. barley or hatcho miso
(or more, to taste)

A popular old-timer with a savory vegetarian twist (skip the hambone!)...

Wash the peas several times, until the water is clear (makes soup less gas-forming). Boil and skim off any foam. Then add seaweed, burdock, onion, and enough water to cover by 1". Cover and simmer 30 minutes. Add other veggies, and just enough water to make desired creaminess. Simmer 30 minutes more. Dissolve miso into soup just before serving.

Healing in the Market

Now, a word of advice...when you shop, keep your senses alert. Fresh, organic foods (that haven't been processed, chemicalized, gassed, dyed, waxed, sprayed, pulverized, whipped, frozen, or emulsified!) have a distinct glow of integrity about them. A spark of quality. If you can learn to recognize <u>this</u> spark, you may soon be able to recognize <u>everything</u> in life that's truly nourishing.

As you start on the produce aisle, look, smell, and touch. Listen for the place inside you that knows intuitively if a vegetable is fresh, or whether a fruit was picked green or allowed to mature.

Take time to hold foods, and ask yourself: "Will this make me feel stronger? Does this <u>feel</u> right?" With trial and error, you'll learn how to avoid glamour and reach for the beauty of substance.

apples
59¢#

If you get mixed messages, that's OK. Life is complex. Pause and evaluate. Get a friend's opinion. A vegetable can <u>look</u> colorful and crisp, but smell of chemicals. Your hunch may tell you it's watery and tasteless. Pay attention to <u>all</u> your senses, then choose in a spirit of adventure.

If you make a mistake, that's OK, too. Next time, it will be easier to choose, just because you took time to feel and evaluate.

Developing a taste for aliveness is a sensitive business-- but it's the most essential business there is.

4 The Self-Healer's Workbook

Need a break from cooking?

This workbook chapter invites you to practice several age-old techniques for preventive self-diagnosis and healing.

First, take a look at the Big Picture, for a holistic overview of complex factors causing your symptoms. (Macrobiotics literally means "a larger picture of life"...macro: large view, bio: life).

Next, study How Symptoms Develop from the perspective of Oriental Medicine, and fill in Prevention Checklists. With new understanding of how your body works, you'll be much more alert for the early warning signals that help you prevent serious illness.

Then, relax with the Inner Balance Exercise, and look ahead, with What to Expect. Healthy eating can catalyze surprising changes in both body and moods. And of course, there may be setbacks, too. Get ready for adventure!

If, however, you're impatient for quick solutions.... you may want to skip this chapter and turn to Chapter 10. There you'll find practical short-cuts to help you lose weight, nourish growing kids, recover from minor illness and more.

When you're ready to know why the shortcuts work (so you can share the good news with family and friends), that's the time to come here and do your homework.

THE BIG PICTURE

Every symptom has a story to tell about your life.

A fascinating story, that can reveal the complex
links between your body, mind, emotions and spirit.

Diet, rushed eating habits, family tensions,
exposure to viruses, work stress, no play, no
time to be creative....All these inter-related
factors can cause symptoms. And many of them
are within your power to change.

But how do you decide what's the most important
factor to change first?

For decades, conventional western medicine has
placed top priority on finding physical solutions
to physical problems. As a result, we have relied on
drugs, radiation, surgery and other high-tech methods
to help us combat and overcome the mysteries of
illness. But these methods are far from 100% effective.

Looking at life through the microscope has, in fact,
kept us from seeing the bigger picture. The whole.

By contrast, many doctors and healers now pioneering
in the field of holistic, preventive health care
are helping patients to see the Big Picture.
Learning from the wisdom of native healers, they
ask: "How's your life?" instead of just "How's
your body?". Then, they listen for the clues
to renewed health, hidden in your story.

Use the following exercise to gain a new, holistic
perspective on your symptoms. For maximum
insight, discuss it with a friend or sympathetic
health professional. Especially watch for
surprises. We are, ultimately, co-artists of
each other's health. We can help each other
change the picture.....

The Big Picture

Check causes you feel are most responsible for your current symptoms.

Then, rate the ones you check, on a scale of 10 (most responsible) to 1 (slight factor).

Rate | ✓ |

past surgery, illness, or injury
inherited physical weakness
past diet (fat, sweet, chemicals, salt, alcohol, etc.)
eating habits (rushed, binges, overeating, etc.)
lack of exercise

emotional stress
suppressed emotions (anger, grief, excitement, etc.)
work stress
low self-esteem

lack of warm, supportive companionship
no play
too few outlets for creativity
hungry for a new life purpose

environmental pollution
exposure to germs & viruses
drugs & medications
aging
concern for the future of the planet

Also consider:

recent positive events which may have thrown you off balance & contributed to symptoms:

romance, marriage, birth, promotion, retirement
sudden success
new strenuous exercise
improved eating habits (causing release of old toxins)
other:

PRACTICAL STEPS YOU WANT TO TAKE, TO CHANGE THE PICTURE:

1. _____

2. _____

3. _____

HOW TO PREVENT SERIOUS SYMPTOMS

In Ancient China, doctors were paid to prevent illness.

Doctor and patient worked as a team, noticing very subtle signs of disharmony in body, mind, and spirit. Whenever the Big Picture needed adjusting, prescribed changes were made with herbs, food, exercise, meditation or prayer, massage, and acupuncture. Prevention was held in such high regard that sometimes if the patient got sick the doctor didn't get paid! (See The Yellow Emperor's Classic of Internal Medicine).

Nowadays, most Americans sense that diet, lack of exercise, and stress all contribute to illness. But we lack a systematic understanding of the development of symptoms which can empower us to take preventive action at the earliest signs of imbalance in our bodies or moods.

The following system, derived from traditional Chinese medicine can help you train yourself in the ancient skill of preventive self-observation.

Study the next few pages on How Symptoms Develop, then use the Prevention Checklists which follow, to see the underlying patterns in your health history.

Once you grasp how your symptoms developed in the past, it will be easier to recognize the next warning signals and adjust your diet and lifestyle to avoid getting sick.

When you really see what's happening, change becomes more possible.

How Symptoms Develop

SYMPTOMS EVOLVE GRADUALLY, IN STAGES
STAGE 1:   Imbalance
STAGE 2:   Accumulation & Discharge
STAGE 3:   Trouble Deep Inside

STAGE 1:   IMBALANCE

All illness stems from imbalance.
Yet the first signs are easy to overlook.
Mild fatigue, nervous stomach, overindulg-
ing in sweets, getting accident prone.
Your body is trying to tell you something....
too much fat, not enough fiber....overworked,
not enough play. But are you listening?

When you're young and fit, the body has a
marvelous ability to correct minor imbalances
and stay healthy. If, for example, you
overeat or eat too many extreme foods, your
body can eliminate the resulting excess toxins,
tension, and energy via many routes: urination,
bowel movements, mucus, sweat, sneezing,
coughing, tears, laughter, talk, sex, exercise,
dreams, creative projects, etc. All these
outlets help restore balance.

But if you continue to eat and live in the
fast lane--always pushing your limits and
ignoring health needs--the body will
gradually lose its self-regulating
capacity.

Eliminative organs get overloaded and
start to function sluggishly. Intestines
clog. Arteries harden. Sinuses and lungs
congest. Emotions flare up, and relationship stresses increase. Eventually, the
immune system falters. Watch out
for Stage 2 symptoms.

Feeling fatigued or
accident-prone? Too
many fats, sweets,
salty foods, or just
plain stress may be
throwing you off-
balance.....For
quick-relaxation, try
the Inner Balance
Exercise on p. 87
to help you pinpoint
the source of trouble.

Ah Choo!

Have chronic hayfever?
Sinus congestion?
Your body may be trying
to get rid of toxins
accumulated from eating
too many rich, fatty,
sweet, salty, and/or
chemicalized foods.
To eliminate toxins via
a better route, see
Gentle Colon Cleanse
Guidelines, p. 189.

STAGE 2: ACCUMULATION & DISCHARGE

What if you ignore the warning signs of
imbalance? Fat, mucus, toxins and tension
can accumulate inside you. This build-up
impairs organ functions and can increase
your susceptibility to illness.

Since the body naturally seeks balance, it
may begin to discharge excesses in new
ways....through hay fever, oily skin, body
odor, skin rashes, colds, flu, diarrhea,
fever, emotional outbursts, etc. Other
common symptoms such as constipation, hypertension, or chronic pain can indicate when
accumulations haven't yet found an outlet.

However, if you have a very hardy body,
you may not get sick during Stage 2.
Instead, signs of mounting inner congestion
may be more subtle....sleepless nights,
stiff muscles or joints, irrational
accidents, deep-held resentment or fears,
rigid mental attitudes.

The Inner Clean-Up Job

Do you need relief from Stage 2 symptoms?
One of the most effective ways to get back
in balance is to simplify your diet.

Eat more whole foods. High-fiber, low-fat,
chemical-free. Gently and powerfully,
these will go to work inside you, helping to:

* reduce cholesterol in the blood
* lower high-blood pressure
* improve blood quality
* discharge excess fat & mucus
* unclog intestines
* release tension & stiffness
* stabilize moods

For cleansing and rebuilding foods that
can benefit specific internal organs,
see Practical Guidelines, p. 184-6.

Prevention Checklists

✓ Check current symptoms

✓✓ Double-check chronic or recurring symptoms

✓ **STAGE 1**

SIGNS OF IMBALANCE

fatigue
nervous tension
mild headache
overeating
indigestion
minor aches and pains
tense or cramped muscles
low sexual energy
feel chilled or flushed
occasional cough or sneeze
itchiness
forgetful, confused
listless, no motivation
mildly depressed
irritable, frustrated
hyper, fidgety
can't relax or unwind
uncomfortable weight gain

✓ **STAGE 2**

SIGNS OF ACCUMULATION & DISCHARGE

bad breath
body odor
sinus congestion
recurring cough or sneezing
oily or dry skin
can't sleep
gas, belching
constipation
diarrhea or loose bowels
vaginal discharge
recurring infections
menstrual tension, cramps
overheat, or perspire easily
hay fever or allergies
skin eruptions (pimple, mole or rash)
recurring headaches
frequent, pale urine
infrequent, dark urine
damp hands and feet
fever
cold or flu
low blood sugar
bingeing
vomiting
mood swings, emotional outbursts
rigid mental attitudes
prone to serious accidents
deep depression, resentment or fear
chronic backache
stiff or painful muscles, joints, spine
high blood pressure
high cholesterol reading
obesity

Prevention starts with seeing the patterns in your health history.

If you only get Stage 1 symptoms, you're coping amazingly well with life on a polluted planet. But if, like most Americans, you frequently get Stage 2 symptoms, it's time to take action to prevent more serious Stage 3 symptoms from developing.

STAGE 3:
COMMON SIGNS OF TROUBLE

chronic digestive upsets
migraine headaches
persistent infections
debilitating pain
cataracts
loss of hearing
loss of memory
insomnia
eating disorders
arthritis
appendicitis
diabetes
herpes
osteoporosis
infertility
impotence, frigidity
hysteria
manic depression
paralysis
kidney or gall stones
cancer
heart disease
other degenerative
   illnesses

STAGE 3:   TROUBLE DEEP INSIDE

What happens if we ignore imbalances daily? And let accumulations mount for years?

Our blood gets sludgy. Organs strain under pressure. And eventually (unless we were born with an exceptionally strong constitution), something inside snaps.

Stage 3 symptoms vary widely...from cataracts and herpes, to diabetes, heart disease and cancer. But underneath the differences, we have one big trouble in common. Through abuse, our bodies lose their natural ability to correct imbalances and resist illness. We have to help them, now.

Food, of course, is a good place to start. A well-planned diet can help to cleanse accumulations, rebuild the blood, and tonify internal organs. See a macrobiotic counselor and take cooking classes to learn which foods are most appropriate for your particular illness. For inspiration, read Recalled By Life, Dr. Anthony Satillaro's story of recovery from cancer on a macrobiotic diet.

However, the gentle power of food can seldom be enough to reverse serious damage to organs and nerves, or to counteract the effect of strong chemicals or drugs. Consult with qualified health professionals and take another look at your Big Picture together. So many interconnected factors affect your health every day. All of them are important.

The following exercise can help you find out, one day at a time, which factors are the most important to change first.

Take your time with it, and really listen to your troubles. Nothing soothes a trouble more than when somebody just listens, and responds with love.

The Inner Balance Exercise

Sometimes, just a very
slight change
in your daily rhythm
can make a big difference
in how you feel....

For the next few days,
plan to pause and
do this exercise
at exactly the time
when you usually feel the most
harried, fatigued, or out-of-sorts.

Take 15 minutes
to go inside
and find your balance-point.
Your center.
All healing flows
from this point.

First, get comfortable. Sit or lie down, and
close your eyes. Let each breath relax your body and mind.
Sink deep. With every exhalation relaxing you more....
count backwards, slowly, from 5 to 1. Breathe out tension.
Breathe in energy. 5...4...3...2...1.

Now, mentally review your day.

Ask yourself: When did I start to feel out of balance?
What were the signs? Let your body remember. Take
your time.......Then, ask why. What caused the imbalance?
(Too much caffeine? Hunger for love? Working too long
without a break?). Let the answer come gently, from
within. Trust that you know the real cause.

Now, ask: How can I restore balance? What small step
am I ready for? Again, take your time....Trust your
inner wisdom to guide you towards a decision that's
energizing, maybe even surprising. Then, count again,
from 1 to 5. Breathe. 1...2...3...4...5. Open
your eyes, and give yourself a hug. You deserve
this kind of gentle attention, every day.

What to Expect

NEW BALANCE IN YOUR MOODS

Diet related moods may be running your life
much more than you'd like to admit.

But once you decide to eat for better health,
even a 3-month experiment with a whole foods
diet can bring the connection between food and
your daily moods into startlingly sharp focus.

With the new self-awareness gained, you can
learn to use food to break free from emotional
ruts, reshape your personality, and become
much more who you earnestly want to be.

Here's how it works. When you start to cut down
on high-stress foods (see p. 38), your body and
moods have a chance to gradually recover their
natural, self-regulating abilities. As your body
sheds fats, stabilizes blood sugar levels, and
releases chronic tensions, you can expect your
emotions to go through changes, too.

You may experience moments--or even whole days--
when you feel newly calm, peaceful and centered.
But look for surprises, too, as your moods and
personality seek new balance. At times, your old
familiar self may suddenly feel like it's turning
into its opposite....("Miss Shy, meet Mrs. Bold!").
Look at the chart below, and see if you can
guess what may be in store for you, as you eat
more healing foods:

The New Mood Swing

IF YOU USED TO BE:	YOU MAY BECOME MORE:
timid & shy	bold & outgoing
always cheery & helpful	serious & introspective
compulsive & hyper	dreamy, enjoy doing nothing
spacy, confused	decisive, authoritative
always thinking & worried	passionate, earthy, sensuous
edgy, irritable, tense	relaxed with risk & adventure

Intrigued? Start a Food/Mood Journal, today. It's
the most effective way to learn more about the links
between food and emotions. When you feel brave, share
what you write, with a friend. Healing changes flow more
smoothly, when you're not trying to make them happen all alone.

Starting a Food/Mood Journal

Find a blank notebook that puts you in the mood
to write. Open it. Then, breathe and relax.
This is your space. As you begin to answer
the following questions, feel free to doodle,
scrawl, make lists, color, write poems, tell
secrets. This is how you'll learn the most
about food and mood.

1. Who am I, throughout the day?

    Describe your typical moods.
    How do you feel on waking? How
    about mid-morning? Bedtime?

2. How am I eating?

    For three days, keep track of
    everything you eat and drink. Be
    sure and read labels (for sugar,
    salt, additives, etc.). Notice if
    you eat mostly processed foods or
    fresh-cooked. Do you eat liesurely,
    or always on the run?

3. Who do I want to be?

    Describe your moods on a typical
    day 5 years from now. What is your
    dream? What are you fueling?

4. How do foods affect me
    and my dream?

    Write or draw how you feel, an hour
    after you eat. Which meals make
    you feel more alive, closer to your
    dream? Which foods/meals leave you
    feeling blah? Speedy or restless?

5. How am I willing to change?

    Start with small steps. Be gentle
    with yourself. Make a plan of action.
    Tell a friend. See p. 135 for ideas
    on Choosing Meals For Your Moods.

Potential Benefits

lower blood cholesterol
better blood pressure
fewer sugar crashes
increased stamina
fewer allergic reactions
more immunity to colds & flu
relief from chronic infection
loss of excess weight
less gas
more regular bowels
fewer aches & pains
wake up more alert
need less sleep
less body & breath odor
softer skin, shinier hair
increased mental clarity
more aware of nature's cycles

NEW BALANCE IN YOUR BODY

Balance is a dynamic, never dull process.

Within 6 months to a year of starting a Self-Healing Diet (see p. 18), you can expect your body to transform itself in many subtle ways. Watch for several signs of progress (see sidebar).

You can expect several, but not all of these benefits. Because your Big Picture is unique. A whole foods diet will affect your body, mind, and spirit differently than anyone else.

Be aware that many Stage 3 symptoms respond quickly to diet, but with some symptoms progress can be slow. Especially when complex factors such as relationship stress, life purpose, chemical therapy, and/or organ malfunction and nerve damage all play a role in causing the symptom.

Health is, however, so much more than relief from symptoms.

It's the courage to persist against odds. The wisdom to trust your own pace. The urge to get up and dance with Mother Nature's challenges.

You can expect the calming power of whole foods to foster these character-building qualities in yourself, too. But you may need a friend's help to see them in yourself....don't be shy to ask!

If no friend's available, and you need an encouraging boost, try this. Put a pot of soup on to simmer, and take time to read Dr. Bernie Siegal's funny and inspiring Love, Medicine and Miracles. Expect to feel better about you.....healing will follow.

LEARNING EXPERIENCES

Of course, there will be tests. In the balancing act of life, healing progress is often followed by setbacks (otherwise known as learning experiences!).

Over-indulging in favorite treats may lead to recurring symptoms...a great incentive to learn moderation (see sidebar).

But, what may not seem fair is that sometimes even healthy eating can cause new symptoms. Here's why.

Whole foods encourage your body cells to cleanse and release stored-up toxins into the blood. If you make a rapid change in diet, your eliminative organs may not be strong enough to get rid of these toxins quickly. Then the body tries to expel toxins through symptoms listed in the sidebar.

Usually, these healing discharges are short-lived. But occasionally, more serious problems such as fatty cysts or kidney stones can be catalyzed by new eating habits.

To Minimize Discomfort & Maximize Learning When Minor Setbacks Occur:

1. Stretch yourself. Continue to research and experiment with healing foods. See Practical Guidelines, pp. 174-5, and the Healing Foods Glossary, p.195 , to learn about helpful foods and home remedies.

2. Respect your Limits. Food can't heal every-thing. If symptoms don't improve, and/or you get fed up with dietary discipline, trust your instincts. It's OK to broaden your food choices and/or focus for awhile on other aspects of your Big Picture (improve family communication, relieve work stress, etc.).

also.....

Possible Setbacks

fatigue
sinus congestion
body or breath odor
excess perspiration
skin eruptions
aches & pains
headaches
nausea
coughing, sneezing
fever
constipation or diarrhea
frequent urination
vaginal discharges
delayed menstruation
emotional outbursts
depression
hypersensitivity

3. <u>Know When to Ask For Help:</u> Listen to your gut
   feelings. You're the only person who knows
   best when your family, friends, doctor, diet
   counselor or other health professionals can
   offer you the nurturing comfort, advice,
   or treatment you need, to recover from setbacks
   quickly. Don't hesitate to reach out and ask.
   (If you don't know who to turn to next.....
   look across the page to <u>A Healing Friend</u>).

IN SUMMARY

A good cook sees the Big Picture of how symptoms
develop, then seasons liberally with prevention.

An even better cook serves up whole foods with a
healthy sense of humor....wisely anticipating that
a self-healing diet will lead both to beneficial
changes in body and moods and to challenging
learning experiences.

The best of cooks knows that we're all in this
mess together. We need to help each other find
what's most nourishing and healing, not only
for our personal ails, but for the planet, too.

This workbook chapter is a humble first step
towards a training manual for such planetary
chefs.

If you have worked hard and used it to
transform your definition of health,
turn the page and reward yourself with
a batch of nummy Sesame Waffles!

A Healing Friend

Finally, if you really want to thrive on a whole foods diet, you'll need friends.

If you don't already have one, take time to imagine one right now.....See yourself walking down a forest path, coming to a quaint, friendly cottage. And in the doorway stands that special person, inviting you in. That kindred spirit who:

EMPATHIZES . . . Says "Yeah, I know what you mean!", while pouring your cup of tea.

AFFIRMS. . . . Sees your uniqueness. Mirrors your strengths. And challenges you, with love, humor, and honesty, to live your dreams.

COOKS . . . . Cooks with you. And for you. Even enjoys your cooking! Ah, that's a friend.

PLAYS . . . . Finds humor, song, dance, and magic hidden in your problems.

EXPECTS THE UNEXPECTED Never has you all figured out. Delights in your surprises.

TRUSTS NATURE'S CYCLES Accepts both ups & downs. Helps you, then asks for help, too.

HELPS YOU PLAN . . Brainstorms. Encourages you to formulate your next steps. Then goes the first step with you.

Write a letter to this imaginary friend in your journal. Become this friend to people you meet. Before long, more than one invaluable buddy will come into your life....eager to join you in using your renewed health to better serve the planet's growing needs.

Sesame Waffles

THE BATTER:

1½ c. oat flakes
1½ c. fine cornmeal
1/4 c. toasted sesame seeds
1/4 c. cooked millet or rice
1/4 tsp. sea salt
2 c. water (approx.)
1 T. sesame oil

* * *

Lightly roast the oats and cornmeal together by stirring in a skillet over medium heat until they smell nutty, but don't brown. Blend sesame seeds to a fine powder in the blender. Add all other ingredients and blend smooth. Ladle into a hot, oiled waffle iron and savor the blissful baking aroma.

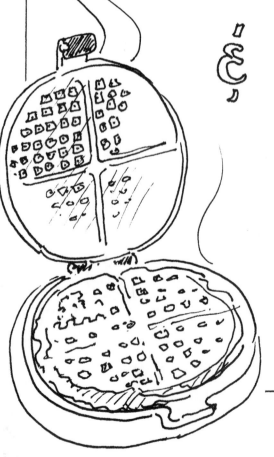

& Apple Syrup

1 c. apple juice
1/3 c. water
1 heaping T. kuzu
2-4 T. real maple syrup (optional)
fresh peaches or berries (optional)

Heat apple juice. Dissolve kuzu in cold water and add gradually to hot juice, while stirring to avoid lumps. Flavor with maple and add optional fresh fruit. If too thick, thin with a touch of apple juice.

Absolutely tastes best served hot.

5 Quick Meals & Snacks

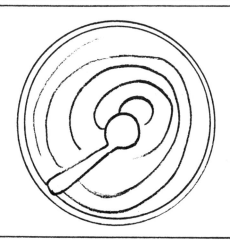

All of us eat some meals in a rush. But our health can go downhill fast if we eat too many high-fat, processed meals and snacks.

This chapter offers you simple, fun recipes to help survive those busy days. Quick breakfasts, satisfying salads, and hearty one-pot-soup-meal (Buckwheat Noodle Soup's my favorite 6 o'clock fix!)

You'll find easy main dishes that bridge to family and friends...like Ginger Baked Fish, Tofu Scramble, and Chinese Vegetables DeLuxe. Plus treats....Spreadables, Sweet Snacks, and Munchies. This may be the chapter you turn to most often, hmmm?

When I'm on a tight schedule, I rely on leftover rice, beans, and steamed veggies (don't have to think!!). But I notice I relax and enjoy my meal more if I take time to thoughtfully season a soup, sauce or salad dressing (see How to Invent Dips, Sauces & Spreads, on p. 109).

Too tired to cook extras? Don't try. Instead, reflect on the following Time-Savers and get organized. There's a calm eye at the center of the whirlwind. Seek it out, and time will nourish you.

Time Savers

1. Cook plenty (enough for tomorrow)

2. Freeze some for emergencies

3. Stock up on fast 'n natural food

4. Pre-wash veggies

5. Cook treats ahead

6. Save steps in an organized kitchen

Time Savers

 Cook Plenty

Make enough grains & beans for 2-3 days. Leftovers can turn into delicious creamy soups, stir-fries, spreads, taco fillings, or lovely rice pudding.

 **Freeze 'Em**

Pre-cooked meal-size portions are great for emergencies (though less vital, with reduced vitamin content). Brown rice gets especially limp after freezing, but many other foods freeze fine, including:

* beans & thick soups
* tempeh
* mochi
* fish
* bread, tortillas, muffins

 **Stock up**

Check out the health food stores for natural fast foods....packaged grain pilafs and soups, frozen tofu entrees, tempeh burgers, tofu hot dogs, fruit-sweetened cookies, etc. But Also keep less-expensive quick-cooking foods handy:

* ramen & buckwheat noodles
* whole wheat & corn noodles
* bulghar wheat
* quinoa & buckwheat
* cabbage, onion, & other roots
* apples, raisins, nuts & seeds

 **Pre-Wash Veggies**

Take time to wash, drip-dry, and store veggies in a crisper when you get home from the store. What a relief to find them crisp and ready to cook when you're in a hurry.

Make treats ahead of time, for the most satisfying meals on busy days. Find a block of time on a weekend or evening and be nice to yourself by cooking up one or more of these:

Cook Treats Ahead of Time

*   bean spread or carrot butter
*   tofu mayo for salad or sandwiches
*   hearty soup to last a couple days
*   vegetable-bean stew
*   cookies or applesauce
*   boiled salad (very refreshing)
*   a noodle, marinated bean or rice salad

Look around your kitchen and ask yourself: "What small steps could I take right away to make cooking more efficient & enjoyable?"

Save Steps

*   <u>Hang favorite pans & utensils</u> on hooks near the stove, where you can reach them with ease.

*   <u>Keep a strainer near the sink</u>, for draining noodles, washing rice and beans, etc.

*   <u>Put a lid rack on top of the fridge</u> to save fishing in a knee-high cupboard 5 times a day

*   <u>Build or install "open" shelves</u>, to make beautiful serving bowls and jars of grains and beans a practical, accessible work of art.

Jot down ideas as they come to mind. Every thoughtful step helps, to streamline meal preparation

Quick Breakfast Cereals

Morning Rice N' Raisins

1/3 c. raisins
½ tsp. cinnamon
1 c. water
2 c. leftover rice
2 T. roasted sunflower
   seeds

Bring raisins, cinnamon and water to a boil. Lay rice on top, cover, and simmer for 5 minutes, then stir. (For creamier cereal, mix rice with ½ c. extra water in blender, then simmer with raisins for 15 minutes). Top with toasted seeds.

Millet or Rice Porridge

2 c. leftover millet
   or rice
2/3 c. water
¼ c. daikon radish,
   red radish or turnip
½ c. leafy greens
miso to taste
or Sesame Salt to garnish

Turnips for breakfast??? Grain and veggie porridge is a staple breakfast in the Orient...light, hearty, and sustaining. Try it, if your energy usually lags mid-morning.

Dice the radish, daikon or turnip. Slice greens. Boil water, add roots and simmer 5 minutes. Add millet or rice and cook 5 minutes more. Flavor with miso to taste, or garnish with Sesame Salt.

Bulghur Sunflower Cereal

3/4 c. bulghur wheat
1½ c. boiling water
¼ c. roasted sunflower
   seeds
pinch sea salt

Make this "instant" cereal before you go to bed at night--it's all ready to eat when you get up.... (great for travellers). Just boil water and pour over bulghur and seeds in a 1 quart wide-mouth thermos. Seal and leave to "cook" overnight. Delicious served with a ladle of miso soup broth...or, for a sweet-tooth, top with amasake.

New Breakfast Options

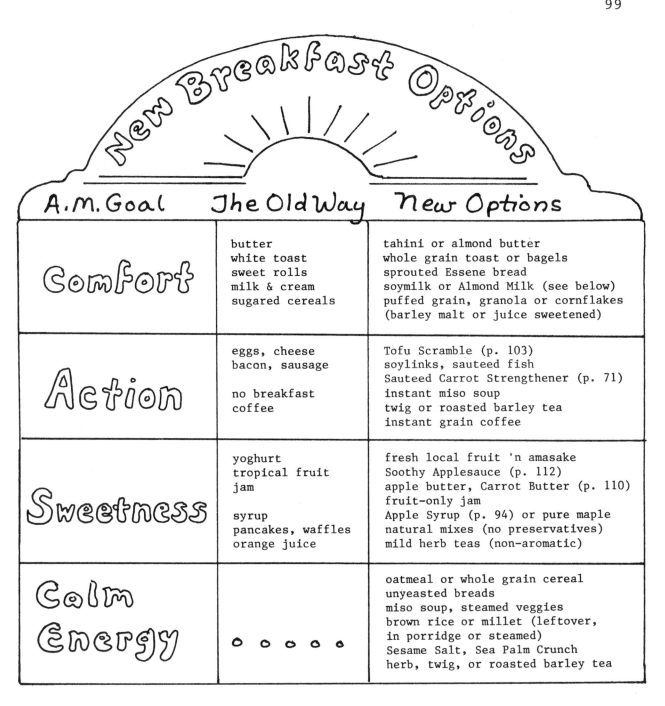

A.M. Goal	The Old Way	New Options
Comfort	butter white toast sweet rolls milk & cream sugared cereals	tahini or almond butter whole grain toast or bagels sprouted Essene bread soymilk or Almond Milk (see below) puffed grain, granola or cornflakes (barley malt or juice sweetened)
Action	eggs, cheese bacon, sausage no breakfast coffee	Tofu Scramble (p. 103) soylinks, sauteed fish Sauteed Carrot Strengthener (p. 71) instant miso soup twig or roasted barley tea instant grain coffee
Sweetness	yoghurt tropical fruit jam syrup pancakes, waffles orange juice	fresh local fruit 'n amasake Soothy Applesauce (p. 112) apple butter, Carrot Butter (p. 110) fruit-only jam Apple Syrup (p. 94) or pure maple natural mixes (no preservatives) mild herb teas (non-aromatic)
Calm Energy	○ ○ ○ ○ ○	oatmeal or whole grain cereal unyeasted breads miso soup, steamed veggies brown rice or millet (leftover, in porridge or steamed) Sesame Salt, Sea Palm Crunch herb, twig, or roasted barley tea

Almond or Sunflower Milk

1/4 c. almonds or 1/3 c. sunflower seeds
1 c. water
1 apple, peeled & diced (optional)

For a non-dairy milk on your cereal,
grind almonds or seeds fine in the blender.
Then add water and optional apple and
blend into a creamy milk. Introduce this
to kids by mixing with milk, to taste.

Lunch Salads

Sunflower Rice Salad

3 c. leftover rice
3 c. boiling water
10 green beans (1" pieces)
1½ c. cabbage (1" pieces)
½ c. carrot, diced small
1 small onion, diced
3 T. minced parsley
3 T. roasted sunflower seeds

A colorful meal in itself! Travels well, packed in a lunch...also popular at picnics.

Briefly boil the beans, carrot, and onion together (2-3 minutes), until just crisp. Lift out with a strainer, drain, and cool. Plunge cabbage in boiling water 1 minute, to barely cook it. Drain and cool. (Save the cooking broth for soups). Toss all together with Lemon Vinagrette Dressing.

Noodle Salad

1 pkg. buckwheat noodles, or
1½ c. corn or wheat elbows
½ bunch watercress, sliced
2 radishes, sliced thin
1 green onion, minced
1 cucumber, peeled & diced

Boil the noodles until just tender, then, before draining, add watercress, radish and green onion. Strain and run under cool water briefly. Toss with cucumber and Tofu Parsley, Creamy Tahini, or Lemon Vinagrette Dressing.

Parboiled Garden Salad

romaine or green leaf lettuce
broccoli, cut in flowerettes
cauliflower, "   "
red radish, sliced thin
green onion, sliced thin
sprouts (optional)

The contrast of crisp, leafy lettuce and crunchy parboiled veggies makes this especially refreshing and digestable. Bring 3 c. water to a boil, then add cauliflower and broccoli and cook 1-2 minutes until crispy-tender. Lift out, drain, and cool. Dip radish and green onion in boiling water for just a few seconds, then drain and cool. Arrange on a bed of lettuce, garnish with sprouts, and serve with any of the following yummy dressings.

Salad Dressings

Tofu Parsley

4 oz. tofu
1 clove garlic
1/3 c. water
1 T. lemon juice
1 tsp. sesame oil
1 tsp. chickpea miso
(or 1/8 tsp. sea salt)
2 T. minced parsley

Steam tofu and garlic for 3
minutes (not longer or it
won't blend creamy). Blend
all ingredients until smooth.
Nice on cooled steamed broccoli.

Sesame Plum

1/4 c. sesame seeds (unhulled)
1 T. brown rice vinegar
1 umeboshi plum
1/4 tsp. dill
1/2 c. water

Wash and drain sesame seeds.
Then roast, by stirring in a dry
skillet on medium heat until
they smell nutty and taste
crunchy. Grind fine in a
blender. Add other ingredients
and blend smooth. Delicious on
Parboiled Garden Salad.

Creamy Tahini

3 T. sesame tahini
1 T. lemon juice
2 T. white or chickpea miso
1/2 c. water
1/4 tsp. basil
1 tsp. olive oil
1/4 tsp. ume-shiso condiment

Mix all ingredients. Especially
tasty on Noodle Salad or
Quick-Boiled Salad (see p. 69).

Lemon-Vinagrette

1/4 c. lemon juice
2 tsp. brown rice vinegar
2-3 tsp. tamari soy sauce
2 tsp. sesame oil (optional)
1/4 c. water
1/2 tsp. thyme or marjoram
2 tsp. fresh minced parsley
1/2 tsp. natural mustard (optional)

Just mix and serve.

Versatile Soyfoods

Tofu:

A soft, white cheese made from soymilk. Bland by itself, tofu readily soaks up flavorings, and can substitute for cheese and sour cream in casseroles, dressings, dips and spreads. Needs to be lightly cooked to be most digestable. Keeps in the fridge up to a week, if you change the water and keep it covered.

Tempeh:

A tangy, substantial soy-patty made from cultured, whole soybeans (more tasty and filling than tofu). High in protein and digestive enzymes. Cook for at least 20 minutes. Saute and add to sandwiches, stir-fries, or spaghetti sauce. Refrigerate up to 2 weeks, or freeze it.

Tofu Mayonnaise

8 oz. tofu
½ c. water
2 tsp. sesame or olive oil
1 T. lemon juice
1 T. brown rice vinegar
1 T. mellow white miso
(or, ¼ tsp. sea salt)
optional sprinkle of dill

Slice tofu and steam for just 3 minutes. Blend all ingredients until smooth and creamy. (This keeps refrigerated for 2-3 days-- if it separates, just re-blend).

Menu Ideas:

*Mix with water-packed tuna for Tuna Salad or sandwiches

*Blend with more water, pickle relish, & grated carrot--Tofu 1000 Island

*Call it Tofu Sour Cream, and serve with bean burritoes or tacos

*Toss with fresh-cooked pasta and steamed veggies for Tofu Stroganoff

*Mix with more, cubed steamed tofu, mustard, chopped pickle,
 and a dash of curry or cumin, for Tofu Egg Salad.

Tofu Scramble

1 carrot, diced very fine
1 stalk celery, diced fine
kernels of 2 ears corn, in season
1 clove garlic, minced
½# tofu
1/3 c. water
1 green onion, sliced
1 T. Italian Herbs, or
2 T. natural salsa (optional)
tamari soy sauce, to taste

Place carrot, celery, optional fresh corn, and garlic in a lightly oiled skillet. Spread tofu on top. Pour in water, bring to a boil, cover, and simmer 5 minutes. Add green onion and salsa or herbs. Flavor with tamari to taste, and simmer a few more minutes without a cover, until any extra water evaporates.

Marinated Tempeh Cutlets

1 pkg. tempeh, cut in 4
1 tsp. sesame oil

Marinade:

1 tsp. ginger juice
1 T. tamari soy sauce
1 tsp. mustard
2 T. water

Quarter tempeh, then cut diagonally to make 8 triangles. Place in oiled baking dish. To make ginger juice, fine-grate ginger and squeeze in your hand over a bowl. Mix marinade and pour over tempeh. Bake 15 min. at 350°. Turn, and bake 10 min. more. Tasty filling for a pita bread sandwich--with sprouts & tahini. Also great with Chinese Vegetables DeLuxe.

Tempeh Peanut Sauté

½ pkg. tempeh
1 tsp. toasted sesame oil
½ c. water
2 c. mustard greens or bok choy
½ tsp. tekka condiment*
or, 2 tsp. tamari
1 tsp. natural mustard
1 c. bean sprouts (optional)
3 T. roasted peanuts

Cut 1/4" slices of tempeh. Saute them in oil, 8 minutes on each side, in a covered pan. Dissolve the tekka and mustard in water, and pour over tempeh. Add greens and peanuts, cover, and simmer 5 minutes. Add sprouts and heat again briefly. Tumble and serve with leftover steamed rice, or ramen noodles.

*Tekka - a savory prepared condiment made from roots & miso...to mail-order, see p. 206.

Meal-in-a-Soup

Fish Soup

4-6 oz. white-meat fish filet
toasted sesame oil
4 c. water
3" strip wakame seaweed,
  cut small
½ c. daikon, halved & sliced
1 c. chopped kale or collards
1 green onion, sliced

FLAVORINGS:

European: ½ tsp. thyme &
marjoram, & sea salt to taste

Japanese: ½ tsp. grated
ginger and 1-2 tsp. tamari

Rub a few drops of oil in a small skillet. Lightly saute fish on medium-low heat until it flakes easily. Set aside. Bring water to a boil in a saucepan, add daikon and wakame, and simmer 10 minutes. Add fish, kale, and flavorings of your choice, and simmer until tender. Add green onion just a few minutes before serving.

Buckwheat Noodle Soup

1 pkg. thin buckwheat noodles
6 c. water
¼ c. carrot
¼ c. daikon or red radish
½ c. broccoli
or, use radish greens or kale
1 green onion
1 c. cooked aduki beans (optional)
miso or tamari soy sauce

Cut all the vegetables in slender, quick-cooking shapes. Boil the water and add noodles, carrot and daikon. Simmer 10 minutes, then add broccoli, or greens, and optional adukis. Cook 5 minutes more, then season with miso or tamari to taste.

Quick Dinners

Chinese Vegetables DeLuxe

2 tsp. toasted sesame oil
1 carrot, sliced diagonal & thin
1 parsnip   "   "   "
1 c. water
1 c. broccoli, cut slender
2 stalks celery, sliced thin
3 c. chopped bok choy or
chinese cabbage
½ c. bean sprouts (optional)
1 more c. water
1 heaping T. kuzu
2-3 tsp. tamari soy sauce

INFINITE VARIATIONS:

Choose the season's pick....
A root, a green,
and always something
sensuous and crunchy....
(try water chestnuts,
pine nuts, or almonds).

A family favorite...especially quick when the kitchen buzzes with the din of many knives chopping.

Warm the oil in a skillet. Saute the roots, stirring over medium heat for a few minutes until they smell savory and start to absorb the oil. Add water, quickly cover, and simmer 5 minutes. Then, add the green veggies, cover and simmer 3-5 minutes until just crunchy. Dissolve kuzu in cold water and stir into vegetables until the sauce thickens. Flavor with tamari to taste.

Serve with noodles, or leftover steamed rice or millet.

Chicken & Ginger DeLuxe

1-2 chicken breasts*, de-skinned
1 tsp. grated fresh ginger
1-2 cloves garlic
1 tsp. toasted sesame oil

*Organically-grown chicken can be enjoyed--in good health--as an occasional delicacy. Worth looking for, it's much preferable to commercial chicken, which often contains growth-hormones and antibiotics harmful to health.

Cooking for a crowd? To make everybody feel welcome...just make a generous batch of Chinese Vegetables and add sauteed morsels of gingery chicken for meat-lovers.

Steam chicken 20-25 minutes, until it pulls easily away from the bone. Sliver, and sauté briefly with ginger and garlic. Add to Chinese Vegetables DeLuxe.

Penny's Fettucine

1 pkg. whole wheat udon noodles
3 cloves garlic, minced
1/2 tsp. toasted sesame oil
¼ c. almonds
1½ c. water
¼ c. leftover brown rice (for cheesy effect, use sweet rice)
2 tsp. mellow white miso
1 tsp. minced celery leaves
½-1 tsp. oregano

One night, in cooking class, Penny was yearning for something quick, creamy, rich and familiar. "How 'bout fettucine?" I said. I didn't know how, but somehow I knew we could create it with the ingredients we had on hand.

Here's what we came up with... everybody agreed, it's a Mom's dream!

While the noodles cook, saute the garlic in oil. Grind almonds fine in the blender, then blend to a cream with water and rice. Add herbs and miso, and heat. Toss with fresh-cooked pasta and serve immediately.

Ginger Baked Fish

6-8 oz. filet of sole, bass, halibut, or red snapper
½ tsp. toasted sesame oil
½-1 tsp. tamari soy sauce
½-1 tsp. finely grated ginger

Rub the fish lightly with toasted sesame oil on both sides. Then, mix ginger with tamari, and rub this on both sides, too. Heat oven to 350°. Place fish in an open skillet and bake for 15-20 minutes until just flaky and tender. Serve immediatly, garnished with lemon and fresh steamed vegetables.

Quinoa Poppy Seed Pilaf

1 c. quinoa
1 onion or leek, minced
3 c. water
2 T. poppy seeds
pinch sea salt
1 carrot, finely grated
1/3 c. minced parsley
1 green onion, sliced

A universal favorite--light, fluffy, and flavorful.

Roast quinoa by stirring in a skillet over medium heat until it smells toasty, but don't brown. Meanwhile, heat water. Just before it boils, add quinoa, onion, poppy seeds and salt. Cover, and simmer 20 minutes. Then, turn off heat, add carrot, parsley, and green onion, and toss to fluff. Let sit 5 minutes to blend flavors. Serve with fish fillets or a side of beans. Or, chill and dress with Lemon Vinagrette.

Burritos for Everybody

To unite family and friends with widely differing tastes, have a serve-yourself Mexican Feast!.....Cook beans ahead. Warm whole wheat tortillas (or taco shells) in the oven. And ask everybody to help lay out a spread of tasty fixins:

THE FIXINS:

BEANS: Pinto, black beans, lentils, or adukis
VEGGIES: Shredded lettuce, scallion, green pepper, sprouts
THE BEEF: Chopped olives, leftover rice, or sauteed ground beef*
CHEESE: Low-salt raw milk cheese or tofu cheese
ON TOP: Homemade Tofu Mayo
ZEST: Natural salsa, sauerkraut, or Sesame Plum Dressing

*For beef lovers: Quality range-fed beef is much preferable to commercial beef, which contains unhealthful growth hormones and antibiotics. Be aware that although beef can give strength, it's also one of the most difficult foods to balance on a whole foods diet. Eat small portions, together with plenty of veggies, or you may find sugar and alcohol irresistable.

Inspired Leftovers

Be fearless and fun-loving! With a little courage
and imagination, that dab of 3rd-day rice could become
part of a cream soup, sauce, cookie, muffin, pilaf, burrito,
pudding, or pie....Go ahead and fool with it!

What to do with Rice

Steam it
Cream it in soup
Layer it in a casserole
Stir-fry it
Roll it up in a tortilla
Mix it in a loaf
Toss in a salad....

And Beans

Make a thick soup
Blend into a gravy
Mash into a spread
Add to vegetable stew
Mix with breadcrumbs, for burgers
Fill tacos or burritos
Refry 'em with onion

#1 Rice Pie Shell
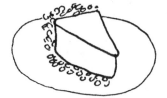

#2 Rice Gravy on Toast

#3 Rice in a Burrito

More Ideas....

1] __SWEET 'N EASY DINNER PIE__ - Press leftover rice in an oiled
pie plate, fill with mashed steamed
yams, and bake til' it's hot.

2] __CREAMED RICE ON TOAST__ -   Steam seasonal veggies. Puree
leftover rice in blender with enough
water to make a thick gravy. Heat,
flavor with miso, and serve as a
sauce over veggies on toast.

3] __SESAME-RICE BURRITOS__ -   Inside a whole wheat tortilla, roll
up rice, steamed carrots & kale (or
cukes in summer), with a generous
slather of sesame tahini & dash of
soy sauce. A great school lunch
or travel food!

How to Invent

Naturally Seasoned Dips, Sauces & Spreads

1] START WITH SUBSTANCE

mashed tofu
mashed beans
blended rice
blended, cooked veggies
or, just water

2] FOR TANG OR ZEST, ADD

brown rice vinegar
lemon juice
mustard (natural)
sauerkraut
umeboshi
garlic
ginger
onion
sweet white miso

3] FOR A SALTY FLAVOR, ADD

sea salt
miso
tamari soy sauce
sauerkraut
ume vinegar
tekka
shiso leaves

4] FOR RICHNESS, ADD

tahini or almond butter
toasted sesame oil
sesame or olive oil
toasted ground seeds
ground almonds

5] FOR A LIGHT SURPRISE, ADD

green onion
minced lemon peel
caraway seed
dill
poultry herbs
Italian herbs
thyme or marjoram
parsley
mirin (cooking sake)

6] FOR A HINT OF SWEET, ADD

rice syrup
barley malt syrup
apple juice
mirin
pureed sweet veggies

** Thicken sauces with kuzu **
Thin anything with water

THREE GOLDEN TIPS:

---

* Add liquids & strong flavors gradually
* Get a friend to taste with you
* Listen together for the "Aha!"

Spreadable Snacks

Sweet Carrot Butter

4 c. carrots, sliced
1/2 c. water
pinch of sea salt
1 heaping T. kuzu,
dissolved in 2 T. water
1-2 T. sesame tahini

Sweet, creamy and super as a spread on whole wheat toast, rice cakes, or even waffles.....

Slice carrots in 1" chunks and place in pressure cooker with water and salt. Bring to pressure, turn down and simmer 10 minutes. (If you don't have a pressure cooker, steam 20 minutes). Puree carrots in blender, with 1/2 c. liquid from pressure cooking or steaming. Dissolve kuzu in cool water, mix with carrot puree, and reheat. Stir until it bubbles (kuzu must be heated thoroughly, to thicken). For buttery flavor, stir in sesame tahini.

Sesame Squash Butter

1 c. mashed, cooked
buttercup or butternut squash
3 T. sesame seeds*
a dash of cinnamon
1 tsp. mellow white or
chickpea miso
water

Carrot butter was my #1 favorite until I invented this! Steam, bake or pressure cook the squash, then mash. Roast sesame seeds by stirring in a skillet over medium heat until they smell toasty and crumble easily between thumb and forefinger.* Grind into a butter in the blender or suribachi. Mix in squash, miso, and cinnamon and add just enough water to make a creamy spread.

*Fresh roasted and ground sesame seeds add a special taste and aroma. In a rush? Substitute tahini.

Bean Spread

2 c. leftover lentils,
    adukis, or garbanzos
1 stalk celery, minced fine
1 green onion, sliced
2 T. minced parsley
2 T. lemon juice
Or, 1 T. brown rice vinegar
2 tsp. miso or tamari soy sauce
¼ c. ground roasted seeds
    (sunflower or sesame)

Toast the seeds by stirring in a skillet over medium heat until they smell and taste nutty (but not too browned, or they'll taste bitter). Grind fine in the blender. Mash the beans. Mix all the ingredients and adjust seasoning to your taste.

Great on rice cakes, whole wheat pita bread, baked brown rice crackers, or bagels.

Hummus

1 c. garbanzo beans
2 c. water
3" strip kombu

1 large clove garlic
1-2 umeboshi plums (to taste)
2 T. toasted ground sesame seeds
(or, use roasted sesame butter)
1/3 c. bean cooking liquid
1 good squeeze lemon (optional)
1 T. chopped green onion

I like to keep a batch of this popular spread in the freezer ...handy for noshers.

Sort through beans for rocks. Wash and soak overnight, then pour off soaking water and add fresh. Pressure-cook with kombu for 50 minutes. Drain beans and reserve cooking liquid.
Steam or lightly saute garlic for a few minutes. Toast seeds and grind (as in recipe above). Combine all ingredients and blend until creamy. Garnish with sliced green onion or sprigs of parsley.

Sweet Snacks

Soothy Applesauce

4 apples
¼ c. raisins
½ tsp. cinnamon
or, ½ tsp. minced lemon peel
1 c. water and apple juice
   (vary mixture to your taste)
1 heaping T. kuzu
2 T. water or juice

VARIATION: Try pears!

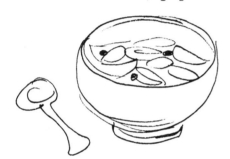

How can it be so simple and taste so good? Like apple pie, without the crust. I marvel while I let the delicate flavor soothe and relax me. What do you think... is the magic in the kuzu, the twist of lemon peel, or the plump raisin?...

Peel, core and slice the apples. Place in a saucepan with raisins, cinnamon or lemon peel, and water. Bring to a boil, cover, and simmer for 10-15 minutes, until apples are tender. Dissolve kuzu in cold water, add and stir until thick. For crunch, top with granola, toasted seeds, or nuts.

Almond Crunch Pudding

THE PUDDING:

1 pt. almond amasake*
3-4 heaping T. kuzu*
 dissolved in ¼ c. water
½ tsp. vanilla

THE CRUNCH:

3 T. chopped almonds
1 tsp. rice syrup

Heat amasake to scalding. Dissolve kuzu in water, add to pudding and stir until thick. (Beat briskly to dissolve any lumps). Add vanilla. Pour into 4 small bowls to cool.

Toast almonds by stirring in skillet over medium heat till browned. Then, put in a bowl, add rice syrup and stir. Cool and sprinkle on pudding.

*AMASAKE - A creamy sweetener made from cultured rice. (It has complex rather than simple sugars--so it digests more slowly than honey or maple syrup--no sugar crash!). Different brands vary in thickness-- experiment to discover how much kuzu you need for desired pudding texture.

Mellow Jello

2 c. apple juice
5 T. agar agar flakes
1 c. fresh strawberries
½ tsp. vanilla
squeeze of fresh lemon
pinch sea salt

MELLOW MINT JELLO: in summer,
omit berries and vanilla. Add
ripe melon & 3 fresh mint leaves.

APPLE WALNUT: in winter, omit
fruit & use only 4 T. agar.
Top with roasted walnuts.

Bring apple juice to a boil with
agar agar flakes*. Simmer 5-8
minutes until agar is completely
dissolved. Turn off heat, stir
in other ingredients, then pour
into a mold or shallow dish to
gel for an hour in the fridge.
(Not instant...but some things
are worth waiting for!)

*Agar agar is a seaweed that
works like Jello. See p. 121 for
more ways to use it.

Yummy Apple Pudding

2 apples
1/4 c. rolled oats
1/2 c. apple juice
1/3 c. water
1/2 c. cooked brown rice
1/4 tsp. cinnamon
1 T. rice syrup
dash of allspice

Peel, core and slice apples.
Lightly roast oats by stirring
in a saucepan over medium heat
until they smell toasty. Add
apples, and other ingredients.
Bring to a boil, cover, and
simmer for 20 minutes. Blend
smooth in the blender. Serve
topped with roasted nuts or seeds.

munchies

Tamari Roasted Seeds

sunflower seeds
or pumpkin seeds
tamari soy sauce

(almonds are great, too!)

Spread the seeds or nuts on a
cookie sheet and bake at 375° for
about 10 minutes, until they puff,
turn golden, and smell very
inviting.

Or, roast them in a skillet,
stirring constantly over medium
heat.

Sprinkle lightly with tamari and
stir until evenly coated. Cool,
then store in a sealed jar in
the fridge, to keep fresh.

The Sauerkraut Snack

leftover rice
a spoonful of sauerkraut
a spoonful of toasted seeds

Would you like to fool your sweet-
tooth? Try eating the opposite
of what you're craving...something
salty and sour.

This combination is great....
crunchy and fulfilling. Just
tumble and munch.

FAT-FREE SNACK OPTIONS:

Rice cakes
Baked Brown Rice Crackers
Mochi (bake it, it puffs!)

For a refreshing change..
try slices of raw
chinese cabbage,
or bok choy.

6 The Intrigue of Sea Vegetables

California Sea Palm

Sea vegetables are the ocean's mineral and vitamin bank--so rich they surpass any food on earth for diversity of nutrients. High in calcium and iron, they also provide B vitamins (including B_{12}), Vitamin A, potassium, magnesium, phosphorus and iodine.

They are an underwater treasure chest of valuable trace minerals: selenium, zinc, copper, rubidium, nickel, and molebdenum. (By contrast, land-grown vegetables now almost totally lack these elements-- so essential for our health--due to modern farming methods which deplete the soil).

Very alkaline, seaweeds help to balance an over-acid blood condition. (From the common cold to cancer, most diseases thrive in over-acid blood). And, in our polluted nuclear age, it's important to know that the brown algae family (which includes kombu, wakame, arame and hijiki) contains alginic acid, which binds and expels radioactive substances and heavy metals from the body.

Are you ready to try them yet? There's one more jewel in the treasure chest....Seaweeds also have calming, soothing effects on the inner sea of emotions. When eaten in small quantities over a period of several months, they can help to calm hyperactive kids, soften and relax rigid attitudes, and enable you to stand up under pressure with ease.

There are many varieties, and they taste intriguingly different....Turn the page to learn how to get started including them in your meals more often.

Friendly Versatility

Next time you find yourself in the kitchen wondering "What do
I really want? What do I need?".....think of sea vegetables.
Often these questions can be your intuition's way of pointing
you in a new direction. Why not turn to the biological source
of all life on earth? Mother Ocean. She offers an amazing
selection (these are some of the most common varieties):

Variety	Unique Quality	Cooking Suggestions:
AGAR AGAR	Gels	A great base (no flavor of it's own) for custards, jello, aspic, & mousses
ARAME	Adds Subtlety	Artful strands give a sweet, briny flavor to casseroles and side dishes with grains & vegetables
HIJIKI	Beefs Up	Robust flavor and bold appearance as a side dish fortify vegetarian meals. Leftovers good in salads.
KOMBU	Tenderizes	Greatly enhances the flavor & texture of beans, vegetables and onion soup.
SEA PALM	Pleases Crowds	Makes a delicious crunchy condiment when roasted & ground with sunflower seeds.
WAKAME	Gently Sweetens	Add to soups, stews, and baked casseroles (makes carrots taste succulent & sweet--like "pot-roast"!)

Seaweeds, Calcium and Iron

Sea vegetables have been widely recommended in macrobiotic reference books as a good source of calcium and iron.

This is true, however one mistake needs to be corrected. Many books state that hijiki contains 10 times the calcium in a glass of milk. This is an error (understandably made by using data which listed the nutrients in dried--not cooked--seaweeds).

As the updated chart below indicates, to equal the calcium in dairy foods, you would need to eat seaweeds and dark leafy greens quite frequently, together with many other whole foods (not all listed) that contain small amounts of calcium.

COMPARISON OF NUTRIENT COMPOSITION OF CALCIUM AND IRON			
Food	**Serving Size**	**Calcium**	**Iron**
Hijiki, cooked	¼ cup	152.6 mg.	3.16 mg.
Wakame, cooked	¼ cup	130 mg.	1.3 mg.
Kombu, cooked	¼ cup	76.4 mg.	0.9 mg.
Tempeh, cooked	3 ounces	129 mg.	10.0 mg.
Milk	1 cup	288 mg.	0.1 mg.
Yogurt	1 cup	272 mg.	0.1 mg.
Sardines, with bones	3 ounces	372 mg.	2.5 mg.
Turnip Greens, cooked	1 cup	252 mg.	1.5 mg.
Collard Greens, cooked	½ cup	145 mg.	0.6 mg.
Mustard Greens, cooked	½ cup	97 mg.	0.65 mg.
Kale, cooked	½ cup ·	74 mg.	1.3 mg.
Broccoli, cooked	½ cup	68 mg.	1.7 mg.
U.S. RDA Calcium: 800-1200 mg., U.S. RDA Iron: 12-18 mg.			

Source of data on Western foods, USDA Handbook #8.

* Chart reprinted from an article by Leonard Jacobs, East West Journal/ May 1985.

The Calcium Controversy

How much calcium do you need? In the world
scientific community, there are widely
differing opinions on that question.

For adults, the USDA recommends 800 mg. daily.
But the World Health Association recommends
600 mg., reflecting the fact that most people
on the planet can't afford or digest high-
calcium dairy foods.

Many prominent scientists, including Dr. Mark
Hegsted, Professor Emeritus at Harvard and
Administer for Human Nutrition under President
Carter, feel that adult calcium needs may be
lower than either of these figures (see
"The Great Calcium Debate", by Kirk Johnson,
East West Journal, October, 1984).

Scientific research confirms that many traditional people who eat a low-calcium diet
nevertheless have very strong bones and teeth
(see Diet and Nutrition, by Rudolph Ballentine).

But other studies show that Americans need
large amounts of dietary calcium--especially
older women prone to osteoporosis. (Other
women's symptoms such as PMS and menstrual
cramps are also linked to calcium deficiency).

Why the discrepancy in the research?

Lack of exercise, high-protein intake, and
a diet high in phosphorus foods (such as soda
pop), all deplete the body's calcium supply.
It's quite likely that subjects of American
studies ate lots of meat and soda pop, and
didn't get enough exercise, and therefore
required much more calcium. But these
variables were not recorded.

But beyond these factors, it may be that
our high-stress lifestyle significantly
interferes with our ability to absorb
enough calcium from our food.

Did You Know?.....

The body's calcium
reserves get depleted
by drinking soda
pop, eating too
much protein, and
not getting enough
exercise. Eat sea
veggies to help
restore these
losses.

Living a more simple lifestyle, and eating
more low-stress traditional foods high in
calcium, vitamins, and minerals (such as
dark leafy greens and sea veggies), may
enhance our ability to extract all the
nutrients we need from our food.

There's no simple answer to the calcium
question. Like so many decisions in this
complex age, we need to base our judgment
on the partial, ever-changing results of
scientific inquiry, together with taking
a broader look at the planetary picture,
and ultimately trusting our own
intuition.

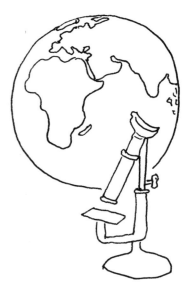

IN SUMMARY

Sea vegetables offer a rich bounty of
nutrients (including trace minerals no
longer available in land vegetables,
due to soil depletion). They have
calming effects on mood and personality.
And when eaten frequently in small
amounts, they can clearly enrich
the calcium and iron in your diet,
and provide a large percentage of
your daily need.

But equally important, for the
natural foods chef, sea veggies are
a great source of sensual pleasure....
offering an array of varied tastes,
textures, and visual effects.
The following recipes continue
the intrigue.

To Weigh Our Calcium Needs...

We must balance info
from western scientific
research (which promotes
high-calcium intake),
with a global perspective
of the health & vigor
of many traditional
peoples who eat a
moderate to low-calcium
diet.

120

Sea Vegetable

RECIPES

Over 75 species are eaten in countries
all over the world--from Ireland to China,
Polynesia and in Native American cultures.

Recipes here are for 8 varieties commonly
available in the U.S. Many have Japanese
names, but some of these are also now
being harvested on our own coasts--in
Maine and California.

If you want a sure winner, try the Sea Palm
Sunflower Crunch, or French Onion Soup
with Kombu.

When you're feeling bold, or want to
feel bold, try hijiki. It'll make your
teeth strong, your hair gleam, your skin
glow, and just looking at it is bound
to improve your sense of humor!

Agar-Agar* - The Jello Maker

A natural gelatin, these white flakes have no taste or
aroma, and simply need to be heated until they dissolve
to make fruit jellos, puddings, or vegetable aspics.
Agar agar provides good bulk for regulating the intestines,
and is also beneficial for losing weight, as it contains
no calories.

CARROT ASPIC

2/3 c. sliced carrot
(1 medium carrot)
1 c. water
3/4 c. chopped greens
(kale, cabbage, bok
choy or watercress)
1 c. water
3½ T. agar agar flakes
3/4 tsp. finely chopped
lemon peel
3 radishes, sliced thin

Cook the carrot in 1 c. water for
8-10 minutes, until soft. Blend
smooth. Bring the other 1 c. water
to a boil, add greens and agar agar
and simmer 5-8 minutes until greens
are tender. Add radishes and
lemon peel and simmer 1 minute
more. Combine all ingredients and
pour into a shallow bowl or mold
to gel. Chill before serving.

STRAWBERRY OR PEACH CUSTARD

6 T. agar agar flakes
3 c. apple juice
1 c. water
2 T. sesame tahini
2 c. sliced strawberries or
fresh peaches
3 heaping T. kuzu
2 T. apple juice
1 tsp. natural vanilla

Bring juice, water and agar agar
to a boil. Simmer 10 minutes.
Stir in sliced fruit and
tahini. Dissolve kuzu in cool
juice. Add to custard and
stir until it thickens. Add
vanilla and pour into dessert
cups to cool and gel. Garnish
with fresh fruit.

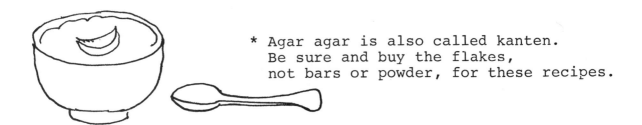

* Agar agar is also called kanten.
Be sure and buy the flakes,
not bars or powder, for these recipes.

Arame - The Artist's Choice

Delicate brown strands with a mild, semi-sweet flavor, and firm, pleasing texture. High in both calcium and iron. Surprisingly artful when combined with other foods--try adding 1/4 c. to a batch of cornmeal muffin batter, or a pot of split pea soup. Also delicious and attractive cooked together with buckwheat and onions as a pilaf. Where else could you use it? Use your imagination!

SWEET CORN & ARAME SAUTE

1 c. arame seaweed
1 onion, sliced thin
kernals from 2 ears corn
3/4 to 1 c. water
toasted sesame oil
tamari soy sauce
rice vinegar (optional)

Wintertime variation:
substitute julienned carrot
for corn

Wash arame (see directions on the next page.) Place in a pot with water. Bring to a boil and simmer uncovered for 5 minutes (it will smell strong at first, then the aroma subsides--this improves the flavor). Then lay the onion on top, cover, and simmer 20 minutes. Add more water as needed to keep arame moist but not submerged--you want most of the liquid to be gone when finished cooking. Finally, add the corn on top, and sprinkle with a few drops of toasted sesame oil. Simmer 10 minutes more. Season to taste with tamari and vinegar.

SAVORY BAKED SQUASH with Arame

1 small buttercup or butternut
  squash
1 onion, halved & sliced
½ c. arame (small handful)
½ c. sliced burdock (optional)
½ c. boiling water
tamari soy sauce

Wash arame (directions on next page). Cut squash in half. Lay flat side on cutting board and peel by shaving down the sides with a sharp knife. Cut in bite-size pieces. Oil a covered baking dish. Layer the arame, onion and burdock in the pot, then add squash and pour in the boiling water. Sprinkle lightly with tamari. Cover and bake at 375° for 45 minutes, or until squash is tender.

To Wash Hijiki & Arame

These two seaweeds need to be washed to remove any sand, dirt, or tiny seashells.

1. First, look for any tiny seashells and remove them. Then, submerge the seaweed in cold water.

2. Rub together and swirl to loosen any sand.

3. Then, lift out of the water, letting any sand settle to the bottom. Place in a saucepan. Discard the wash water.

HIJIKI needs to be soaked before cooking. Cover with fresh water and soak for 10 minutes or until pliable. Use soaking water in cooking.

ARAME doesn't need soaking (even if the package says otherwise--it tastes better without soaking). Just let it sit a few minutes to absorb the wetness from washing before cooking.

Hijiki - The Strong One

Striking black strands, with a firm texture and uniquely strong flavor. Richest of all the seaweeds in calcium and iron--a good choice when you need to be able to stand up under pressure. Known in Japan as "the bearer of wealth and beauty", hijiki is traditionally used to strengthen the bones, revitalize skin and hair. Also builds strong intestines.

JULIENNED CARROTS & HIJIKI

1 c. hijiki
1½ c. water
1 carrot, cut julienne
a few drops toasted sesame oil
1 tsp. rice vinegar (optional)
½ tsp. tamari soy sauce

Measure (approximately) 1 c. hijiki and place in a bowl. Submerge with water and wash (see directions on p. 123). Discard the washing water, then soak in 1 c. fresh water for 10 minutes.

Bring to a boil, then cook uncovered for 5 minutes. It will smell strong at first, but the aroma subsides--this improves the flavor.

Add the other ½ c. water, cover, and simmer for 20 minutes. Then add carrot on top and simmer 20 minutes more. Season to taste, with tamari, toasted sesame oil, and vinegar. Simmer a few more minutes to blend flavors.

Serve small quantities, warm or cooled, as a side dish.

Add leftovers to noodle or rice salads, soups, or casseroles.

Kombu - The Great Enhancer

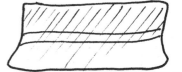

Mellow flavored, broad green frond, expands greatly when
soaked. Contains glutamic acid--a food tenderizier and flavor-
enhancer. Softens beans and makes them more digestable.
Sweetens root vegetables in stews, so they melt in your mouth.
For "al dente" kombu, cook 1/2 hour to 45 minutes, then slice
into bite size pieces or julienne strips. Or, cook it for 1½
hours in a pot of beans, stir the pot and the kombu will dissolve
and dissappear.

FRENCH ONION SOUP with Kombu

6" strip kombu
2 lg. dried shiitake mushrooms
1 onion, halved & sliced thin
4 c. water or stock
3 T. tamari, or to taste

Soak the mushrooms in ½ c. water
for 10 minutes, then slice them
thinly. Place in a pot with soaking
water, kombu, onion, 2 T. tamari,
and the rest of the water. Bring
to a boil, cover, and simmer 20 to
30 minutes. Remove the kombu
(save it to add to a pot of beans
or rice). Adjust seasoning to taste
with tamari. Serve garnished with
fresh parsley.

MELLOW ROOT STEW with Kombu

6" strip kombu
1½ c. water
1 onion
1 carrot
1 parsnip or turnip
1 stalk celery & leaves
2 cabbage leaves
1 heaping T. kuzu
2 T. cold water
tamari soy sauce to taste
½ tsp. basil or thyme (optional)
½ c. diced seitan (optional)

Place kombu and water in a pot and
bring to a boil. Cover and simmer
20 minutes, then remove kombu,
slice in ½" squares, and add back
to the pot. Cut all the veggies in
bite-size wedges or slices. Add
onion, roots and celery to kombu and
simmer 15 minutes. Then add cabbage
and simmer 5 minutes more, or until
everything is tender. Dissolve
kuzu in cool water, and stir this
into the stew until it thickens.
Flavor to taste with soy sauce and
optional herbs. For meaty heartiness,
add chunks of seitan....a savory
high-protein wheat gluten product.

Nori - The Sushi Wrapper

Paper-thin sheets of pressed seaweed with a mild, distinct ocean flavor. Crispy when lightly toasted. Good source of protein and Vitamin A. Most often used as a wrapper for sushi-- a picnic or party hors d'oeuvre filled with brown rice and vegetables. (Sushi in Japanese means any food artfully rolled up and served with a tangy seasoning).

NORI "POCKET" SUSHI

4 sheets of nori, toasted
Fresh cooked brown rice
Several lightly steamed, colorful vegetables cut in strips:

broccoli
carrot
crookneck squash
celery
scallion
radish greens
etc.

Fingers of sauteed tempeh or tofu

Here's a sushi variation that guests can participate in creating right at the table. Toasted nori squares (a sheet cut in 4), are hand held like tacos, filled with rice and colorful steamed vegetables. Drizzle a tangy sushi sauce on top.

To toast nori: Wave it over a gas burner on low heat (or electric burner on medium) until it gets crispy and changes color to a uniform light green. Cut in quarters.

Sauce: Combine equal parts of lemon juice, mellow white miso, and water. Add a dash of brown rice vinegar to taste.

Serve vegetables, tempeh or tofu, and sauce on a platter. Toasted nori and rice in separate bowls. Let guests make their own "Japanese tacos"!

Sea Palm — The California Native

Savory tasting, small green fronds, native to California.
Delicious and crunchy when roasted and ground as a condiment
(almost everybody likes this!). It has a softening effect,
similar to kombu, when added to stews and soups. For an
unusual snack, try munching on it raw--it's kind of like
beef jerky.

SEA PALM SUNFLOWER CRUNCH

1 oz. package of sea palm
½ - 1 c. sunflower seeds
(use the larger amount for
a less salty condiment)

Roast the sea palm on a cookie sheet
in the oven for 10-15 minutes at 350°,
until crispy but not browned. Roast
the seeds at the same time, on a separate
sheet so you can take them out if they
get done first--they should be golden
and puffed, but not brown. Crumble
the sea palm into a suribachi and
partially grind, then add sunflower
seeds and grind together to a chunky
texture. Serve as a condiment on
grains or vegetables. Store in a sealed
jar in the fridge to keep it fresh.

SWEET PARSNIPS 'N SEA PALM

1 small onion
2 parsnips
½ c. sea palm (small handful)
½ tsp. sesame oil
½ c. water (approx.)
½ tsp. tamari soy sauce
or , 1 tsp. white miso
optional dash of mirin
(cooking sake)

Cut onion in half by cutting from end-
to-end (not across the middle). Slice
in slender half moons. Cut parsnip
in half lengthwise, then slice in
long diagonals. Saute together in
oil, stirring for a few minutes
until fragrant. Then add sea palm,
cut in small pieces, and pour in
water. Quickly cover, and simmer
20 minutes. Water should be all gone
at the end of cooking. Season with
soy sauce, or miso and mirin. Enjoy.

Wakame - The Women's Seaweed

Graceful, green fronds with a subtly sweet flavor and
slippery texture. Expands quite a bit, so cut it in small
pieces. High in calcium, thiamine, niacin, and Vit B_{12}.
Traditionally used in Oriental medicine to purify the blood,
strengthen intestines, skin, and hair. Beneficial for the
reproductive organs, and to help regulate women's cycles.

ONE-POT LENTIL DINNER with WAKAME

6" strip wakame
1/3 c. lentils
2 c. short-grain brown rice
1 stalk celery
1 parsnip or carrot
1 onion
pinch of rosemary or thyme
2 pinches sea salt
5½ c. water

Cut the wakame in small pieces.
Wash the lentils and rice. Cut the
vegetables in small compatible shapes.
Layer everything in an oiled baking
dish with a tight cover. Add water,
bring to a boil on the stovetop, then
bake at 375° for 1 hour.

While dinner cooks itself,
Enjoy yourself!

Butternut Stew with Wakame

3" strip wakame
2 c. water
4 c. cubed butternut squash
1 onion, cut in 8
1 small burdock root, sliced
1 c. cooked garbanzo beans
1 T. tamari
1 stalk celery, sliced
1 c. diced cabbage
1 tsp. mirin

A sweet & hearty one-pot meal....
Soak wakame in water, while you
peel & cube squash, cut onion &
slice burdock. Cut wakame in small
pieces, then place in pot with
water and bring to a boil. Layer
onion, burdock, squash and beans in
the pot, cover and simmer 15 minutes.
Sprinkle with tamari, then, without
stirring, add a layer of celery &
cabbage. Cover and simmer 10 min.
Add mirin and stir. Serve with
thick sliced rye, or cornbread.

SESAME-WAKAME SPRINKLE

1½ T. roasted wakame powder
(approx. 1 pkg. wakame)
½ c. roasted sesame seeds

Roast wakame on a cookie sheet in the oven, 10-15 minutes at 350°, until crisp but not browned. Roast seeds on a separate sheet until they smell nutty and crumble easily when rubbed between thumb and forefinger. Break off the stiff mid-ribs of the wakame and save these for soup--they have sharp edges which don't grind down. Crumble the rest of the wakame into a suribachi and partially grind, then add sesame seeds and grind together until seeds are partially crushed. Serve as a garnish for grains, vegetables, or thick soups. Keep in a sealed jar in the fridge.

Wild Nori - The Crinkly One

Crinkly, delicate flavored, native California Nori--in loose, leafy form. A good source of protein and Vitamin A. Low in sodium. Crispy when fresh roasted, it turns firm and chewy when it gets moist again.

WILD NORI CRISP

Spread one package of wild nori on a cookie sheet and roast in a 350° oven for 5-10 minutes, until it turns lighter brown or green and feels crispy. When cool, crumble. Store right away in a tightly sealed jar to keep it crisp. Serve as a low-salt condiment with grains, beans, or soups.

The Serving Exercise

You've probably already imagined the responses you may get from family and friends if you serve them seaweeds. All of us have mixed feelings about change....and somehow, seaweeds bring them all up!

Watch for the signs. Noses wrinkle at the name. Eyebrows lift as the fork lifts. Fannies wriggle.

Before things progress too far, you can help your guests by talking about your own mixed feelings. How did you feel when you were cooking the strange wiggly stuff? Check the following list for possible feelings:

proud of yourself for risking
embarrassed
scared to taste
fascinated
tender
sneaky
resentful (of the new responsibilities of self-healing)
appreciative (of the benefits)
righteous
dedicated
pioneering
alone
ridiculous
awkward
loving

Reflect on your list, share a little of your mixed feelings, then invite your guests to do the same.

Seaweeds can actually be great icebreakers, when you want them to be.

7 Rotating Foods For Health & Pleasure

It's September in my garden. Green beans abound.
My mouth waters for the ripening sweet corn. Winter
carrots slowly set down their tender roots. And
Big Sweet Mama Squash dries on the vine. She'll be a
treat in February, and conversation piece 'til then.

A breeze brings the smell of apples. Kale, collards
and broccoli unfurl their leafy coats, getting ready
for frost. I'll wait to pick, until they're strong
enough to resist snow (fresh greens in January
remind me I can make it through the cold, too!).

In my garden, I'm rediscovering how natural and
rewarding it is to eat different foods in each season.
Every morning I traipse out in my slippers to see
what's new. By the time I eat, I'm savoring a
relationship. Ah, such fulfillment....
Every day, something a little bit different,
delectable and beautiful emerges from the cooking
pot. My family's changing moods feel nourished
with the changing seasons, too.

Sound appealing? This chapter shows you how to bring
nature's garden variety right into your kitchen
and your life, through meal rotation:

THREE BASICS OF MEAL ROTATION

* Break free from ruts, with local seasonal foods
* Eat different foods each day, based on how you feel
* Clarify goals & plan meals that help you reach them

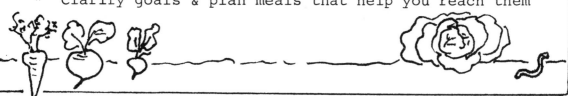

Meal rotation can
help you break:

The Fast Food Rut
The Meat & Potatoes Rut
The Diet Soda-Candy Rut
The Coffee & Donuts Rut
The No-Breakfast Rut
The Fruit & Yogurt Rut
The Chips & Cheese Rut

Why Break Free From Ruts?

Did you grow up eating in a rut? Most of us did (see sidebar).

Even if you succeed in switching to whole foods, chances are, you'll still tend to go on automatic and plan repetitive meals. (Are you already headed for a Brown Rice-and-Miso Rut?).

There's danger, however, in turning to any food out of habit. You risk getting out of sync with the natural world, which is ever-changing and flowing around you.

The body vibrates with nature's rhythms and yearns for whole foods variety. If you always gravitate towards refined, processed foods (even so-called healthy ones, like rice cakes), you stop the process. The immune system falters. And you may get sick.

The immune system's job is getting rid of everything that doesn't belong inside you. That's a big job, in our excessively consumption-oriented, polluted society. No wonder immune system diseases such as AIDS, allergies, and yeast infections are on the increase.

Rotating a variety of foods--especially foods which help to cleanse and strengthen your internal organs in each season--is one sure way to lighten the load on your immune system and build a bank of resistance against illness.

On the following pages, you'll find a systematic way to get started, with 5 Basic Meal Plans and sample menus. These are based both on 5 Element Theory from traditional Chinese Medicine, and on my own research with a wide-range of American families making a change in diet.

Renewing Your Organs With Seasonal Foods

Long ago, the ancient Chinese discovered that
our internal organs respond in very specific ways
to seasonal changes in weather and diet.

For example, the kidneys--which often get stressed
by cold winter weather--can be strengthened by
eating aduki beans (especially the Hokkaido variety,
which keep their vital red color and hearty flavor
all through the winter).

In every season, particular foods stimulate ki--
or vital energy--to flow through a pair of
inter-related organs (see below). Every year,
the cycle repeats itself...Mother Nature's
plan for building lifelong resistance
to illness.

To learn more about foods beneficial for
each organ pair, turn the page.

ORGANS TO NOURISH IN EACH SEASON:

SPRING	Liver / Gall Bladder
SUMMER	Heart / Small Intestine
LATE SUMMER	Spleen-Pancreas / Stomach
FALL	Lungs / Large Intestine
WINTER	Kidneys / Bladder

*Kidneys, not pictured, are located behind
 the liver & stomach, next to the spine.

Lungs   Heart   Lungs

Liver   Stomach   Spleen

Pancreas

GALL
BLADDER

Large Intestine

Small
Intestine

Bladder

Seasonal Healing Foods

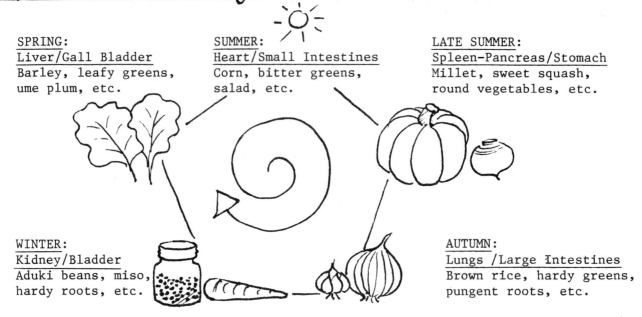

SPRING:
Liver/Gall Bladder
Barley, leafy greens,
ume plum, etc.

SUMMER:
Heart/Small Intestines
Corn, bitter greens,
salad, etc.

LATE SUMMER:
Spleen-Pancreas/Stomach
Millet, sweet squash,
round vegetables, etc.

WINTER:
Kidney/Bladder
Aduki beans, miso,
hardy roots, etc.

AUTUMN:
Lungs /Large Intestines
Brown rice, hardy greens,
pungent roots, etc.

During each season, you can give your organs a boost
by emphasizing healing foods. Even out of season,
foods listed above may benefit stressed organs.

To monitor internal organ health, listen to your
changing moods (the mini-seasons of your daily life).
Positive moods indicate vigor. But negative moods
can signal weak, sluggish, or overactive organs.
Here's an example of how your moods, organs, and
the seasons are closely interlinked:

In Spring, outdoor exercise and gardening send
oxygen-rich blood to the liver, stimulating it to
cleanse winter's fats. The result...you feel
great! But if you're stuck indoors--in an airless,
temperature controlled office--you may feel
restless, impatient, or even short-tempered.

In any season, feelings of irritability can be
lifted by eating more spring greens....bok choy,
mustard greens, collards, chinese cabbage, etc.
Cut down on winter warming foods (pressure-cooked
grain, oil and nuts, salt, animal food, baked foods).
Soothe yourself, instead, with a light Barley Mushroom
Soup. When the weekend finally comes, you'll feel
light enough to enjoy it.

See the 5 Basic Meal Plans and sample menus which
follow, to learn how to rotate meals for
every change of season and mood.

Choosing Meals for Your Moods

IF YOU FEEL:	AND YOU WANT TO FEEL:	CHOOSE THIS BASIC MEAL
anxious worried too sympathetic too sensitive think too much	calm soothed more discriminating more self-determined like singing	#1 The Soothing Millet Meal for spleen-pancreas/ stomach
sad depressed lethargic can't think clear	relieved more compassionate energized more organized decisive	#2 The Reliable Rice Meal for lungs/ large intestines
afraid overwhelmed confused lack confidence	courageous know your own mind self-confident committed	#3 The Hearty Meal for kidneys/ bladder
impatient restless frustrated intense angry resentful	more patient alert self-expressive assertive less angry clearer	#4 The Clean-Tasting Meal for liver/ gall bladder
overexcitable too tense unable to enjoy life like a workaholic	more relaxed playful lighter inspired celebrative	#5 The Relaxing Meal for heart/ small intestines

☑ Check how you feel and want to feel, then choose a
Basic Meal Plan.

Detailed menu plans are listed on the next 5 pages.
Use them as guidelines, but please feel free to
follow your own intuition and improvise, too. Creative
leaps enhance the flavor and healing power of any
simple food.

#1 The Soothing Millet Meal

BASIC OPTIONS

Millet
Sweet Rice or Mochi
Garbanzo or Aduki Beans
Sweet Squash or Roots--
    carrot, parsnip, etc.
Round, Compact Veggies--
    turnip, cabbage, etc.
Arame or Kombu
Sesame Salt
Kuzu Sauces & Puddings
Kuzu Tea (see Glossary)

MOOD EFFECTS

To soothe yourself

Calm down

Feel fulfilled

BODY EFFECTS

To reduce sweet cravings

Regulate blood sugar

Settle an upset stomach

A COMFORTING BREAKFAST

Millet Porridge
Whole Grain Toast
or Evolving Cornbread
(made into muffins)
Sweet Carrot Butter
Twig Tea

SOOTHING SUPPER

Mellow Root Stew
    with Kombu
Pot-boiled Millet
or
Pressure-cooked
    Sweet Rice
Sesame Salt
Almond Crunch
    Pudding
Roasted Barley Tea

LATE SUMMER PICNIC

Hummus
Whole Wheat Pita Bread
Sweet Corn & Arame
Steamed Cabbage
 & Rutabaga
Mellow Jello
Hawthorne Berry Tea (cool)

TRY: MILLET BURGERS * VANILLA MILLET PUDDING *   MILLET MASHED POTATOES

Late Summer seasoning is comforting and.....

Sweet

#2 The Reliable Rice Meal

BASIC OPTIONS

Miso or Tamari Soup
Brown Rice
(short or long-grain)
Wild Rice
Lentils, Fish, Tofu
  or Tempeh
Sturdy Greens & Roots
Seasonal Squash
Varied Sea Vegetables
Toasted Seeds & Nuts
Ginger, onion, garlic
Seasonal cooked fruits

MOOD EFFECTS

To think clearer

Be more decisive

Get organized

Feel compassion

BODY EFFECTS

To regulate intestines

Tone Lungs

Cleanse blood

Increase stamina

SUSTAINING BREAKFAST

Miso Soup
Lundberg's Rice Cream
Sea Palm Sunflower Crunch
Roasted Barley Tea

WORKING WOMAN'S LUNCH

Leftover rice and
Marinated Tempeh Cutlets
rolled in a whole wheat
tortilla with
steamed watercress, sprouts,
mustard or sesame tahini

QUICK SUPPER

Cream of Broccoli Soup
Tofu Scramble or Bean Spread
Toasted Sourdough Bread
Twig Tea

FANCY SEAFOOD DINNER

Miso Soup w/ crookneck squash
Ginger Baked Fish
Pressure-Cooked Rice
Steamed Kale
Sesame Salt
Daikon Condiment (see p. 196)
Julienned Carrots & Hijiki
Apricot Mousse
Grain Coffee

Autumn Seasoning is energizing and....

PUNGENT

#3 The Hearty Meal

BASIC OPTIONS

Miso or Tamari Soup
Aduki or Black Beans
Buckwheat*, Barley, Oats
Pressure-Cooked Rice or
    Millet
Buckwheat Soba Noodles*
Seitan
Kombu, Sea Palm or Hijiki
Sturdy Winter Squash,
Greens & Roots
Pickles & Salty Condiments*
Low-Fat Baked Desserts

MOOD EFFECTS

To feel self-confident

More independent

And courageous

Know Your Own Limits

BODY EFFECTS

To strengthen kidneys*
    & bladder

Restore energy

Renew sexual vigor

2 SUPER WARMING BREAKFASTS

Buckwheat Noodle Soup
Mochi
Twig Tea

*

Overnight Oats
Steamed Kale & Carrot
Sesame Salt
Lotus Tea

A HEARTY MAN'S SUPPER

Winter Simmer
Aduki Beans
Pressure-Cooked Rice
Steamed Collard Greens
Tekka (see Glossary, p. 201)
Apple Crisp
Grain Coffee

Winter flavors are warming and moderately....

Salty*

* A Note of Caution: Kidneys may be too
contracted if you have overeaten salt and
animal foods in the past (infrequent, scant
and dark urine is a signal). If so, avoid
buckwheat and minimize salt. Eat more
greens and fat-dissolving vegetables.

#4 The Clean-Tasting Meal

BASIC OPTIONS

Barley, rye or wheat
Quinoa
Radish, Turnip or Daikon
Lightly Salty Miso Soup
Cabbage & Leafy Greens
Lentil, lima or navy bean
Shiitake Mushrooms
Wakame or Nori
Sauerkraut, Lemon,
Umeboshi, Pickles
Fennel, Caraway Seeds

MOOD EFFECTS

To feel patient

Calmly assertive

Flexible

Alert & Clear

Creative

BODY EFFECTS

To cleanse liver &
   gall bladder

Reduce cholesterol

Dissolve fat & mucus

Help relieve hay fever &
   pre-menstrual symptoms

SPRING TONIC SOUP (for 1)

Brocolli
Turnip Greens or Bok Choy
Parsley
Green Onion

Very finely chop 1½ cups of
of mixed, fresh spring greens.
Heat 1 c. water, add greens,
and simmer for 5 minutes
only. Puree in the blender.
Sip this incredibly green
brew for a light breakfast
or supper. Then go do yoga,
jog, or garden in the
Spring air....Your liver
will love you!

STEAMED RYE HORS D'OEUVRES

Slice unyeasted rye bread thinly.
Quarter each piece. Place in
steamer for 3 minutes. Serve
warm, with a spoonful of
sauerkraut and sprinkle
of caraway seeds on
each piece.

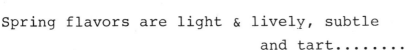

Sour

Spring flavors are light & lively, subtle
                    and tart........

#5 The Relaxing Meal...

BASIC OPTIONS

Pot-boiled Brown Rice
(short or long-grain)
Corn or Cornmeal
Wheat or Corn Noodles
Tofu, Pinto, Kidney,
Black or Barbanzo Beans
Summer Veggies & Salad
(lettuce, cukes, green
beans, sprouts, etc.)
Nori and Sea Palm
Desserts with cooked
 fruit, amasake, or
 rice syrup

MOOD EFFECTS

To feel lighter

Playful

Celebrative

Inspired

BODY EFFECTS

To relax the heart*

Relieve stress

Loosen tight muscles

FESTIVE ITALIAN NIGHT

Whole Wheat Spaghetti
with Marinara Sauce
Par-boiled Salad with
Lemon Vinaigrette
Strawberry Custard

GREAT PICNIC LUNCH

Sunflower Rice Salad
Hummus
Whole Wheat Pita Bread
Steamed Watercress
Mellow Jello
(with fresh peaches)

DELICIOUS LIGHT BREAKFAST

Fresh Corn Chowder
with
a big spoonful of
leftover millet
Red Clover Tea

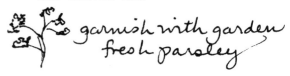
garnish with garden fresh parsley

*A Note of Precaution: These menus
may not be appropriate for
serious heart conditions...see
Kushi, Diet for a Strong Heart.

The taste of summer is juicy, happy, and
refreshingly....

Bitter

Signs of Healing

As you experiment rotating these Basic Meal Plans, watch for encouraging signs:

ORGANS	SIGNS OF HEALING
Spleen-Pancreas/ Stomach	Less heartburn and indigestion More immunity to colds & infection Fewer sugar cravings
Lungs/ Large intestines	More regular bowels Breathe deeper, sinuses clearer Less body & breath odor
Kidneys/ Bladder	Less lower back pain Stay warm easier Urine beer-colored (not pale or dark) Healthier hair Less water-retention
Liver/ Gall Bladder	Sleep better Less indigestion & gas Mid-back more relaxed Skin clearer, less dry or oily
Heart/ Small Intestines	Lower cholesterol levels Chest, neck & shoulders more relaxed Complexion less red

Over the course of many seasons, as you eat more locally-grown whole foods appropriate for your needs, your whole body may come to feel more at ease with nature's rhythms. You'll shiver less in winter, sweat less in summer, settle down more eagerly in fall, and burst out of your cocoon quicker in spring.

If you have serious symptoms, however, food alone may not be enough to stimulate renewed health. Many other healing disciplines can complement enlightened meal planning....including acupressure, acupuncture, herbology, yoga, psychological counseling, meditative visualization, chiropractic and holistic medicine. Trust your intuition. Research and reach out in new directions. They are all linked.

A Conscious Splurge

Do you have a secret urge to wolf down foods that aren't included in these Basic Meal Plans? If so, next time you head for a 12" pizza, an ice cream binge, or a rice cake rampage, try this:

Shift your frame of mind and slow down. Let yourself truly relish this splurge. Forget about guilt. Focus instead on the tastes. The textures. The emotional comfort and release.

It's quite natural, in this process, to notice some things you don't like about the food you're eating, too. If these become overpowering, however, stop. And look for another food you like better. (Part of the purpose of this exercise is to let yourself really take in pleasure. Surprisingly few people know how to do this).

Eventually, the pleasure will subside. When that happens, ask yourself one question....

What in life could be even more fulfilling than this pleasure? Don't try to find an answer. Just ask, and wait. In the right time, now or later, the answer will come to you..... Thank the food for helping it come.

IN SUMMARY

The most energizing diet is one which increases your sensitivity to the natural world. 5 Basic Meal Plans in this chapter (based on the 5 Element Theory from Chinese medicine) can help you cultivate this sensitivity, by cooking to stabilize your moods and revitalize internal organs, in rhythm with the changing seasons.

Seem complex? Maybe you need to step back and enjoy a conscious splurge. Then, turn to the following Refrigerator Chart for a succinct overview.

My favorite Hearty Autumn Stew recipe concludes this chapter. Try it some night when you're in the mood for fulfillment.

☆ Mood Food ☆

FEEL..... BUT WANT TO FEEL.... COOK.......

FEEL	BUT WANT TO FEEL	COOK
overwhelmed afraid cold	self-confident capable warmed	miso soup aduki beans black beans buckwheat soba noodles roots & greens winter squash
impatient frustrated	alert decisive creative	barley rye or wheat lentils white beans spring greens daikon
tense dramatic	relaxed playful joyous	corn or quinoa tofu pintos garbanzo beans salad & veggies local fruit low-guilt treats
worried oversensitive self-conscious	calm centered giving	millet sweet rice garbanzo or aduki beans sweet squash sweet roots
stuck sad depressed	energized relieved clear	brown rice tempeh lentils roots & greens miso onion, scallion ginger

✳ ✳ ✳ REFRIGERATOR CHART ✳ ✳ ✳

© The Self-Healing Cookbook

Hearty Autumn Stew

A WELL-ROUNDED MEAL IN ONE POT

4 c. water
1 lg. carrot
1 c. daikon radish
1 onion
1 stalk celery
½ c. burdock root
or parsnip (optional)
2 c. butternut squash
1 strip kombu
1/2 pkg. tempeh
1/2 tsp. sesame oil
1/2 c. fresh peas
2 heaping T. kuzu, in
¼ c. cool water
sea salt to taste

Peel the squash and cut the vegetables in friendly, bite-size shapes. Slice tempeh in 1" squares, & saute, covered, in an oiled skillet on medium-low heat, 10 minutes on each side. Meanwhile, boil the water, add seaweed, onion, daikon, squash, carrot and burdock. Simmer 20 min. then add sauteed tempeh & celery. Simmer 20-25 minutes more, & toss in the peas. Remove kombu, slice into small squares, and return it to the pot. Season to taste. with sea salt. Add kuzu & stir until thick. Stir well, so some of the squash dissolves into a creamy, thick sauce. Yum!
Serve in bowls.

This slow-simmered, tasty stew goes over big with hearty eaters. Be sure and make plenty! Serves 3-4.

8 Low-Guilt Desserts

High-pleasure, low-guilt desserts are easy to concoct with natural ingredients. The secret? Start by reminiscing....

Take a minute to relax and imagine a video-tape of your life running backwards. Stop at the most mouthwatering, ultimately satisfying dessert from your past. Check out its most memorable qualities (see sidebar).

This chapter guides you in choosing the most delicious, healthy ingredients that can give you these qualities, minus the undesirable after effects. Recipes are coded, so you can choose ones most appropriate for your needs.

Enjoy 'em...And watch for the warm glow, after indulging. Naturally sweetened, low-fat desserts are much less likely to bounce you around than conventional, high-fat, sugar-laden treats. And much more likely to bring out the true sweet tenderness in you.

> MY MOST
> MEMORABLE DESSERTS:
> ✓
> creamy & cool
> crunchy
> sinfully rich
> fresh & fruity
> warm & crumbly
> layered
> decorated
> gooey
> chewy
> topped with goodies
> full of morsels

THE 3-STAR DESSERT CODE

* most gentle

** richer + sweeter

*** enjoy in good health, but watch out for drama!

Wholesome Tips

For desserts that will love your body as much as you love them:

1. <u>COOKED LOCAL FRUITS</u> - Are less expansive than fresh fruits, and less stressful on kidneys, liver, and intestines.

2. <u>ROASTING FLOURS & OAT FLAKES</u> - Makes them more digestable and brings out their best flavor. (Use fresh ground flours whenever possible, and store them in the fridge to retain vitamin content).

3. <u>FOR A BUTTERY FLAVOR</u> - Use unrefined corn oil in pie crust or cookies.

4. <u>ADD WHOLE COOKED GRAINS</u> - For filling, satisfying desserts that "stay with you", add leftover rice, millet or oats to puddings. Or, substitute a cooked grain for part of the flour in cookies or sweet muffins.

5. <u>IF YOU GET GAS EASILY</u> - Avoid combining fruit & grain in desserts. Make a Sweet Squash Pie, Almond Crunch Pudding, or Creamy Rice Pudding (minus the raisins).

6. <u>TO MELLOW OUT</u> - After an especially sweet and rich dessert, come back to earth with twig tea or roasted barley tea.

7. <u>OVERDO IT?</u> - Have some soothing kuzu tea (see Healing Foods Glossary, p. 200)...it will calm your belly <u>and</u> your sweet-tooth!

Choosing Your Just Desserts!

	HIGH DRAMA * * *	MILDER CHOICE * *	MOST GENTLE *
SWEET:	sugar molasses	honey maple syrup	apple juice rice syrup barley malt syrup
CHOCOLATEY & GROWN-UP	chocolate coffee alcohol	carob	grain coffee
RICH:	butter lard refined oils	tahini sesame, corn & safflower oil	unrefined sesame oil (small quantities)
NUTTY:	cashews coconut	almond, walnut, sesame butter other local nuts	roasted sesame seeds & sunflower seeds, chestnuts
CREAMY:	cream & milk sour cream cream cheese	almond milk natural yogurt tofu & soymilk	creamed oats rice nectar (also called amasake)
CUSTARDY:	cornstarch	arrowroot	kuzu
FRESH & FRUITY	pineapple banana dates figs mango	locally grown fruits--fresh dried, juiced, or cooked-- peach, cherry, berry, lemon, apricot, etc.	especially apples, or try sweet-tasting vegetables: carrot, parsnip, winter squashes

The Chooser's Code:

*   Gentle, Low-Guilt Effects

* *   Medium Effects (richer & sweeter)

* * * Ah! Everybody needs one of these sometimes!

(Look for stars on the recipes that follow....)

Easy Puddings

Vanilla Millet Pudding *

2 apples, peeled & sliced
1¼ c. water
½ tsp. cinnamon
1 tsp. vanilla
1 T. chopped raisins
1 T. sunflower seeds
1½ c. leftover millet
1 heaping T. kuzu,
dissolved in 2 T. cold water
2 T. rice syrup

In a saucepan, layer the chopped raisins, apples, cinnamon, sunflower seeds, and leftover millet. Pour in water, and without stirring, bring to a boil. Simmer 10-15 minutes, until apples are tender. Dissolve kuzu in water, and add to pudding with rice syrup and vanilla. Heat and stir until it thickens

Creamy Rice Pudding *

1 c. amasake (almond flavor)
½ c. water or apple juice
2 c. leftover rice
3 T. chopped raisins
3 T. sunflower seeds
or, chopped roasted nuts
1 tsp. cinnamon
or, grated lemon peel
1 tsp. vanilla (optional)

Combine all the ingredients except vanilla. Heat and simmer with a flame spreader underneath for 10-20 minutes. The longer you cook it, the softer it gets. Delicious served warm.

AMASAKE is a mild, creamy sweetener made from rice and a culture. Look for it in the fridge at the health food store. For the simplest pudding, simply heat amasake by itself, and thicken with a little kuzu dissolved in water.

Two Apple Favorites

Apple Crisp **

TOPPING:

½ c. barley flour
1½ c. rolled oats
2 T. corn oil
¼ c. rice syrup
½ c. sunflower seeds
2 T. chopped walnuts
1/8 tsp. sea salt
½ tsp. cinnamon

FILLING:

8-10 apples (Jonathon,
    Rome or Granny Smith)
½ c. raisins
½ tsp. vanilla
2/3 c. apple juice
1/3 c. water
1 heaping T. kuzu

Lightly roast flour & oats together, by stirring in a skillet over medium heat until heated through, but not brown. Quickly remove and put in a bowl, so it doesn't burn. Heat oil and rice syrup, then pour over oats and flour. Add seeds, nuts, salt and cinnamon, and mix well.

Peel and thinly slice apples (squeeze a little lemon on 'em to keep from browning). Spread apples in a 9 x 12 baking dish. Dissolve kuzu in juice and water, heat and stir until thick. Drizzle over apples, then crumble topping on top. Bake at 350° for 30-40 minutes, until it bubbles.

Baked Apples *

2 large apples (Rome,
Pippin, Granny Smith or
Jonathan work best)
1 T. roasted sunflower seeds
1 T. raisins
¼ tsp. vanilla
¼ tsp. cinnamon
2 tsp. water
sesame oil

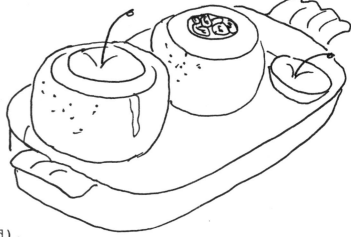

Slice off and save the tops of the apples (as illustrated). With a small knife or apple corer, hollow out 1" in the center of each apple, being careful not to poke through the bottom. Mix all the other ingredients and fill the apples. Replace the top slice of apple, and bake at 375° for 30-45 mintues until tender. For juicier apples, cover halfway through cooking.

Chewy Oatmeal Cookies

Oatmeal-Raisin Cookies *

1¼ c. oat flakes
½ c. raisins or currants
3/4 c. water
1/8 tsp. sea salt
1 tsp. cinnamon
2 T. sesame oil
½ c. whole wheat pastry flour
½ c. leftover brown rice
3 T. sunflower seeds
3-4 T. rice or barley syrup

Everybody has a favorite cookie texture. I like these because they're chewy and moist. (If you like 'em more crunchy and dry, try the 2nd recipe).

Lightly roast oats by stirring in a skillet over medium heat. Boil water and pour over oats and raisins, and let sit 10 minutes. Mix in salt, cinnamon, oil, and rice syrup. Then add flour, rice, and seeds. Shape by the spoonful into round, flat cookies on an oiled baking sheet. Bake 25 minutes at 375°.

Walnut Oatmeal (wheat-free) **

2 c. oat flakes
¼ c. rice or barley flour
½ c. oat flour
¼ c. sesame oil
½ c. raisins
1/3 c. chopped walnuts
1/4 tsp. sea salt
1 tsp. cinnamon
pinch allspice
1/3 c. rice syrup
2/3 c. water
1 tsp. vanilla

Here's one for kids who are allergic to wheat....Looks and tastes like the real thing--Mom's oatmeal cookies!

Roast oats by stirring in a skillet over medium heat until they're hot, but not browned. (This brings out the flavor and makes them more easily digestable). Lightly roast flours. Combine wet ingredients and stir vigorously. Add dry ingredients. Let dough set 5 minutes, to stiffen. Shape into 2" round cookies, on an oiled cookie sheet (press flat with the back of a spoon). Bake at 350° for 20-25 minutes.

BARLEY MALT SYRUP

Party Cookies

Maple Sandies ***

3 c. whole wheat pastry flour
1½ c. rolled oats
1/2 tsp. sea salt
3/4 c. chopped toasted almonds
1/4 c. maple syrup
1/4 c. barley malt syrup
1/3 c. unrefined corn oil
2 tsp. vanilla
1/3 c. water (approx.)

Combine flour, oats, almonds and salt. In a separate bowl, mix wet ingredients. Stir together, and moisten with water to make a dough that holds together without being too sticky. Shape into rounds or squares, and press down lightly to flatten, on an oiled cookie sheet. Bake 20 minutes at 350°. Great holiday cookies!

Date Nut Softies ***

2 c. oat flakes
1/2 c. chopped dates
1/2 c. almonds
1 c. amasake
pinch sea salt
1/2 tsp. vanilla
1/4 tsp. grated orange peel
12 almonds (to decorate)

Yummy Raisin Variation:

substitute 1/3 c.
monukka raisins for dates

Irresistably soft, chewy & sweet!

Roast oats in a skillet, stirring over medium heat until they're hot, but not browned. Rub oats and dates together. Then, whiz in the blender ½ c. at a time, till thoroughly blended. Place in a bowl. Grind almonds to a powder in the blender. Mix all ingredients (dough will be quite moist). Oil a cookie sheet. Shape into twelve 2" round, flat cookies. Press an almond in center of each. Bake at 350° for 25 minutes. Keep refrigerated (if they last!).

STILL ATTRACTED TO THE SUGAR PLUM FAIRY?....Try a cookie sweetened with maple syrup or dates......

Pie Crust

Nutty Oat Crust **

3/4 c. oat flakes
3/4 c. whole wheat pastry flour
1/4 c. brown rice flour
1/4 c. chopped walnuts
2 T. sesame oil
1/4 tsp. sea salt
1/3 - 1/2 c. water

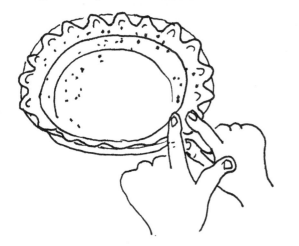

Lightly roast the oat flakes, then the flours, by stirring in a skillet over medium heat until they smell toasty, but don't brown. Mix in salt, walnuts, and oil, with a fork. Add just enough water that it hold together when you squeeze a little, without being sticky.

HOW TO MAKE A PRESSED CRUST:

Spread crust mixture evenly in a pie plate. Begin in the center and press into a thin crust, pushing the extra to the sides, then up, to form a rim. Flute the edge, as illustrated. For squash pie, bake for 10 minutes at 350°, then fill and bake 25 minutes more. For fruit tarts or cream pies, pre-bake 20 minutes at 350°, cool and fill.

Wheatfree Oat Crust *

1 & 1/3 c. oat flour
2/3 c. brown rice flour
1/4 tsp. sea salt
2 T. sesame oil
2/3 - 3/4 c. water

To make oat flour, whiz rolled oats in the blender. Roast flours, combine ingredients, press into pie plate and bake as in directions for Nutty Oat Crust, above.

Millet Crumble Crust *

3/4 c. millet flour
1/3 c. cornmeal
3/4 c. whole wheat pastry flour
1/4 tsp. sea salt
2-3 T. corn oil
1/2 - 2/3 c. water

Make millet flour by grinding millet on high speed in the blender. Roast flours, combine ingredients, and press into pie plate as above. Bake for 20 minutes at 350°. Wonderfully delicate and crumbly with a fruit or cream filling.

Fresh Fruit Pies

Peach Pie **

4 c. fresh sliced peaches,
or, apricots, pears, nectarines
blueberries or cherries
2 c. apple juice
2 T. agar agar flakes
2½ heaping T. kuzu, in
1/2 c. water
1 tsp. vanilla
pinch sea salt

Arrange peaches or other fresh fruit on a pre-baked Millet Crumble Crust. Bring juice and agar agar to a boil, then simmer 5 minutes. Add kuzu, dissolved in cool water, and stir until thick. Add vanilla. Cool a few minutes, then pour over fruit. Let set for an hour in fridge before serving.

Strawberry Pie **½

3 pints strawberries
1/2-3/4 c. rice syrup
1/2 c. agar agar flakes
1 heaping T. kuzu, in
2 T. apple juice
1/2 tsp. sea salt

Indescribably sweet & tart-flavored. Wash and de-stem the berries and sprinkle them with salt. Place in a pot, and turn on low heat (no need to add liquid-- the fruit quickly makes some). Drizzle rice syrup and sprinkle agar agar on top. Cook 15 minutes, stirring once in a while. Dissolve kuzu in apple juice, then add to berries and stir until thick. Cool briefly, then pour into a pre-baked crust (Nutty Oat, Wheatfree Oat, or Millet Crumble). Gel for 3 hours at room temperature, or 1 hour in the fridge.

Holiday Pies

Sweet Squash Pie *

3 c. cooked, mashed squash
(buttercup or butternut)
½ c. water
2 heaping T. kuzu
¼ tsp. sea salt
2-4 T. rice malt syrup
1½ tsp. cinnamon
¼ tsp. allspice (optional)
pinch of nutmeg & cloves

My all-time favorite mellow pie....
especially with a garden-grown sweet
buttercup squash.

Cut the squash in quarters and remove
seeds. Then, either place in an oiled
covered baking dish and bake at 400°
for an hour....or, place in a steamer
basket inside a pressure cooker with
3/4 c. water and pressure cook 20
minutes. Peel and mash, then puree
in blender.

To make filling, dissolve kuzu in
water (or, use cooled liquid from
pressure cooking). Heat and stir
vigorously--to prevent lumps--while it
thickens. Add pureed squash, rice syrup
and spices. Fill a partially baked
Nutty Oat or Wheatfree Oat Crust and
bake 25 minutes at 350°. Cool before
serving.

Chestnut Cream Pie **

1 c. dried chestnuts*
1 c. water
2 c. amasake
¼ c. almonds, ground
1 tsp. vanilla
1 tsp. cinnamon
pinch allspice
2 T. agar agar flakes
¼ c. chestnut cooking liquid

*Dried chestnuts can
be purchased in
oriental markets.

This one's as rich and creamy as
cheesecake...but with a very mild
"sweet effect".

Soak the chestnuts overnight in water,
then pressure cook for 1 hour. Drain,
and reserve cooking liquid. Grind
almonds fine in the blender. Add
amasake, chestnuts, vanilla and
spices, and puree until creamy.
Heat agar agar with chestnut
cooking liquid until thoroughly
dissolved--about 5 minutes. Stir in
the chestnut cream. Pour into a
pre-baked pie crust. Let cool and
set for an hour in the fridge before
serving.

Cream Pies

Lemon Dream Pie ✻

PIE FILLING (or pudding)

2¼ c. plain amasake
1½ c. apple juice
1½ tsp. grated lemon peel
3 T. agar agar flakes
pinch sea salt
3 heaping T. kuzu
1½ T. lemon juice
1 tsp. vanilla
1 T. rice syrup (optional)

For a sensuous treat....
top with fresh raspberries

Lovely, light & subtle....

Heat amasake, juice, agar agar and lemon peel. Simmer 5 minutes, 'til agar dissolves. Mix kuzu with lemon juice (and add a dash of apple juice until it dissolves). Add to pot and stir until it thickens. Add salt & vanilla. If too tart, add rice syrup. Cool briefly, then pour into a pre-baked crust (Nutty Oat, Wheat-free Oat, or Millet Crumble). Let set for 1 hour in the fridge before serving.

Chocolate Cream Pie ✻✻✻

1 c. chocolate amasake
1-1/4 c. chocolate soymilk
2 T. agar agar flakes
2 T. kuzu
1 T. arrowroot
2 T. cool water

4-5 oz. silken tofu
1/4 c. chocolate soymilk
1 T. grain coffee powder
3 T. agave nectar (light)*
1 tsp. vanilla
1/3 c. chopped walnuts
2 squares of an organic
   chocolate bar, grated

*Ask your local health food
   store to stock agave--
   a mild and pleasant
   sweetener made from
   the cactus plant.

This fancy pie brings smiles!. . .

Simmer amasake, soymilk & agar 8 minutes or 'til agar melts. Dissolve kuzu and arrowroot in water. Whisk hot mixture while you drizzle in kuzu. In blender, combine tofu, soymilk, coffee, agave and vanilla. Blend smooth. Whisk this into the hot pudding, then pour into a pre-baked Nutty Oat Crust (or, into a glass pie plate--it's great on it's own!). Cool 1 hour. Decorate with a ring of nuts & chocolate shavings.

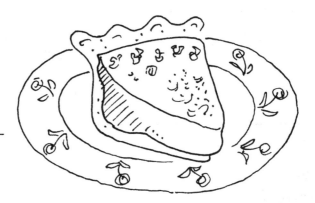

Just Scrumptions

Apricot Mousse **

1/2 c. dried apricots
1 c. apple juice
1 c. water
1/4 c. agar agar flakes
2 heaping T. kuzu, in
1/4 c. apple juice
1 T. rice syrup
1 T. sesame tahini

Variation:

for extra rich, thick mousse
double the apricots

Bring apricots, water, juice, and
agar agar to a boil. Cover and
simmer 10 minutes. Dissolve kuzu in
cool juice. Add to pot, stirring
until it thickens. Pour into blender.
Add tahini and rice syrup and blend
until creamy smooth. Pour into
a shallow bowl, small pie plate,
or pudding cups to cool. Garnish
with toasted seeds or an almond.
Serves 6.

Strawberry Couscous Cake **

Cake:

1 c. couscous*
1½ c. almond amasake
½ c. water
¼ c. apple juice
pinch sea salt
1 tsp. vanilla

Topping:

1 c. halved strawberries
2/3 c. apple juice
1 heaping T. kuzu
½ tsp. grated lemon peel
½ tsp. natural vanilla

This appealing easy no-bake cake
rivals strawberry shortcake!

In a saucepan, combine couscous,
amasake, water, juice, and salt.
Heat and stir for 10 minutes, or until
couscous swells and becomes soft.
Add vanilla. Pour into a cake pan,
smooth the surface, and add topping.

Topping: Arrange strawberries on
top of cake artfully. Dissolve kuzu
in juice, add lemon peel, heat and
stir until it thickens. Add vanilla.
Pour over strawberries and cake.
Let cool for an hour in the fridge
before serving.

*COUSCOUS is a partially refined
wheat product that fluffs up
quickly when added to liquid.

Homemade Mochi *

Do you have an incurable sweettooth, by now?

MOCHI, a traditional Japanese New Year's treat made from
glutinous sweet rice, may be just what's needed, to
bring your tastebuds gently down to earth.

Mochi is delightfully sticky, chewy and subtly sweet.
More than any food, I credit mochi with giving me the
whole-grain satisfaction that enabled me to get unhooked
from a lifelong sweet addiction. (I grew up eating ice cream
almost every night after dinner, hiding chocolate chip
cookie dough under my bed.....)

Store-bought mochi is ultra-convenient. It comes in many
flavors. You just pop it in the oven looking like a brick,
and it puffs up into a wonderfully crunchy snack.

But homemade mochi is an experience to rival the old-fashioned
ice cream freezer. On special occasions, I like to gather
some friendly folks and share the fun:

THE DOWN-HOME MOCHI RECIPE:

2 c. sweet brown rice
2 & 1/8 c. water
pinch sea salt

Decorations:

raisins
cinnamon
pumpkin seeds
sesame seeds
sunflower seeds

If you <u>really</u> want
to break a sweet habit,
decorate them with
cooked aduki beans--
surprisingly tasty.

Wash & drain rice. Pressure-cook
by starting it on a low flame for
30 minutes. Then turn to high and
bring up to pressure. Reduce heat
to simmer, put a flame spreader
underneath and cook 20 minutes more,
then let it come down from pressure
on its own.

Gather your friends round, now,
and turn the steaming sweet rice
into a big suribachi. Take turns
passing the bowl and pounding as it
gets sticky and taffy-like. When
everybody agrees it's done (the smooth-
er the better), turn the oven on.

Make cookie-size shapes and press
them flat onto a well-oiled cookie
sheet. Decorate, then bake at °400
for 20-30 minutes, until puffed
and crispy on top. Eat 'em hot!

Nana's Apple Cake

My Nana's kitchen smelled of cinnamon,
and she served a cozy apple cake for dessert.
I think of her mother in Kentucky, and her mother in
Europe, baking this simple cake to celebrate harvest time.
May you and your family enjoy it fresh and warm,
topped with a drizzle of fragrant Cashew Cream.

1-1/2 c. whole wheat flour
1/2 c. unbleached white flour
1 tsp. baking powder
1 tsp. baking soda
1/4 tsp. sea salt
1/2 tsp. cinnamon
1/8 tsp. nutmeg
1/8 tsp. cloves

1/2 c. raisins, chopped
1-1/2 c. boiling water
2 c. apple, diced small
1/4 c. almonds
1/3 c. safflower oil
3 T. brown rice syrup
1 T. maple syrup
juice squeezed from
   1 T. grated fresh ginger
2 tsp. vanilla

Sift together dry ingredients.
Pour boiling water over chopped
raisins and set aside to cool.
Steam diced apple 5 minutes.
Grind almonds in the blender
to a fine powder. Add raisins,
water, oil, sweeteners, vanilla
and ginger juice. Blend until
smooth. Mix wet with dry
ingredients, gently folding in
the apples.

Pour into an oiled 8" square
glass cake pan. Bake at 350
degrees for 40 minutes, or until
an inserted toothpick comes
out clean.

Cashew Cream

1 c. raw cashews
3/4 c. water
1/8 tsp. fine grated lemon peel
1-1/2 tsp. vanilla
2 tsp. maple syrup

A wonderful dairy-free topping for natural desserts!
Soak cashews in water for an hour or more.
Place all ingredients in the blender,
and blend until creamy smooth.

  Celebrating

Congratulations! Changing your eating habits
is hard work. And whether you have made big
changes or little ones, you deserve to relax and
reward yourself, your family, and friends, with
a scrumptious feast.

How can you relax and make a whole foods feast at
the same time? If you're a sensitive person, you
probably feel nervous introducing new foods to family
and friends--especially on holidays. And you're not
alone if you don't like the thought of spending extra
hours cooking on special occasions.

Three strategies can help you get past the worries
and enjoy the event.....

1] Keep it artful and simple

2] Or for a splendid feast, plan to cook with friends

3] Have fun with being different

<u>Artful and Simple</u>

Think minimal. Which simple foods please you
the most? What <u>little</u> pleasures would you enjoy
sharing with your guests? Just one artful taste
on a holiday can transform everybody's ideas of what's
possible with natural foods. Finding that taste
can be exciting. (Turn the page for a few of my
easiest holiday successes).

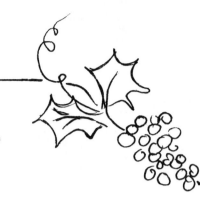

Easy Celebrative Food Art

For a Wedding Potluck

A platter of SESAME RICE BALLS
(Lovingly hand-rolled balls of
Pressure-cooked brown rice--
Coated with toasted sesame seeds.)

What people said:

"How novel!"

"Just rice? It's so tasty!"

For A Family Reunion Dinner

SUPER-SWEET BUTTERCUP SQUASH
Steamed and mashed with cinnamon,
Topped with roasted, fresh walnuts,
and warmed in the oven.

"But it's so sweet!"--both
my cousin and my sister-in-law
were surprised it didn't have
any added sweetener. I was
tickled to give them such a
simple recipe

For A "Finger-Food Luncheon"

SAUTEED TEMPEH "FINGERS"
Marinated in tamari, ginger juice,
And a little vinegar,
Rolled in a steamed collard leaf,
Rubbed with toasted sesame oil.

"These are good ....."
What are they??"

"Who made these things?
I don't know what they are,
But I like 'em!"

To invent your own, pause and imagine:

A texture that melts in your mouth
An aroma that comforts or excites you
The season's freshest, sweetest flavor
A playful form
A special name

Coordinating a Feast

Hungry for a feast that bridges differences
and unites you with family and friends? Here's
how to cook it up....pause first, and ask yourself:

"What mood do I want to create in the kitchen?"

Warm, clear, and peaceful? Spontaneous, light,
and playful? Let the answer bubble up in its
own time. Then, recruit co-workers who will be
the most excited about your idea. Here's
several ways you could do it:

Plan Together

With a friend, decide on the mood and menu
you want. Then ask each guest to bring a
specific dish that fits your theme. Great
for international meals or Thanksgiving.

Cook Together

For a luscious spread with compatible dishes
like Millet Mashed Potatoes, Stuffing, Gravy,
Sauteed Tempeh, Salad, and Almond Crunch
Pudding....Prepare special ingredients ahead
of time (such as wild rice for the stuffing).
Then, invite a crowd to meet early, and cook
together in teams. The common agreements....
To taste as you cook, until both cooks say
"Aha! Mmm!" or "Yes!" Ask for dishwashing
volunteers before you eat!

Celebrate Eating Together

A time-honored tradition in many cultures....
start or conclude the meal by eating one
dish ritually--as a symbol of the occasion.
Tell a story. Really taste your unity.

Finally, Take Time Just For You

Before you cook...run around the block, or
dance in the kitchen. In the middle...stop
for a 10 minute nap! After it's over....
have a cup of tea, or sing a song in the
dark. Drink in the quiet like precious
liqueur.

(A hint for contented
co-workers.....
Greet them with tools
and ingredients laid
out as artfully as
if you were setting
the table. This
makes cooking much
more enjoyable!)

Celebrating Differences

It takes courage to be outwardly different.
(Although, almost everybody feels different
inside). And face it, when you risk cooking
healthy for holidays and social occasions,
your differentness is going to be out there
in the open.

Seem scary? If you simply fret about it,
your food choices probably will become the
uncomfortable focus of attention. But there's
another, much more enjoyable option....

You can use your new eating habits as a spring-
board for entertainment, to bring you closer
to family and friends. Be light-hearted or
profound. Spoof yourself. Sing a song or
read a poem about you and food. In your own
magic way, help people to celebrate something
we all have in common...how different we
each feel.

At the same time, cook to nourish yourself
(make food that sounds inviting, looks friendly,
and tastes great to you). You may be surprised
how many people ask for a taste (or seconds!).
Let me tell you a story about all this....

The Christmas Rutabaga

ONE CHRISTMAS, Rich and I started our Christmas dinner
in an unusual way....by passing two bowls around our
circle of friends.

First, came slices of fresh, steamed rutabaga.
Then, an inviting mound of creamy tofu dip.

"Friends", I said, "these are rutabagas. Please take a
slice and hold it while we honor this strange food."
Linda giggled. "I know this is a different way to
start Christmas dinner. But that's the point.
Rutabagas are willing to be different.....So different,
that Rich can't remember their name".....

(cont.)

"For 2 years, every time I cooked a rutabaga, Rich would predictably hold up a slice and say, 'Now, what's this?' Now, he not only likes 'em, he grows 'em..." I turned to Rich with a twinkle in my eye.

"We offer you these rutabagas from our garden..." said Rich, "as a symbol of our gratefulness for your growing friendship. Especially your willingness to join us in being just a little different. We <u>like</u> that about you all." More giggles. And eyes twinkling. Some glowing.

"But here's the dip!" I said. "Dunk your root to your heart's content, and taste the familiar. The creaminess that makes differences more palatable and friendly." The bowls went round amidst more giggles, a guffaw, and moments of pregnant silence.

"Ah," said Linda. "This is good." We grinned. The bowls went round twice, and all the morsels vanished in a lick. Somebody, I don't remember who, said "I never ate a rutabaga before....it's kinda sweet"... And so our Christmas began.

IN SUMMARY

Keep it artful and simple. Risk doing what's on your heart. Chances are you'll make it so intriguing to cook together that your family and friends may volunteer to help you organize another feast.

The following favorite recipes remind me of my childhood American-style holidays.....
I hope you enjoy them!

RECIPES:

<u>Burgers & Gravy</u>
Buckwheat Burgers
Sesame Gravy
Millet Burgers
Tofu Mayo
Black Bean Gravy

<u>Surprisingly Italian</u>
Marinara Sauce
Tofu Ricotta Sauce
Tofu Pizza
Lasagna

<u>Festive Salads</u>
Crispy Cabbage-Dill
Rice Wedding Salad

<u>Holiday Feasting</u>
Brown Gravy
Millet "Mashed Potatoes"
Savory Stuffing

<u>Evolving Cornbread</u> -
like Mom's spoonbread

Burgers & Gravy

Buckwheat Burgers

1 c. cooked buckwheat
1½ c. cooked garbanzo beans
1 stalk celery, minced fine
2 T. finely minced parsley
1 green onion, sliced
½ tsp. marjoram
½ tsp. thyme
½ c. sourdough breadcrumbs
1 tsp. tamari soy sauce
approximately ½ c. water
1/2 tsp. toasted sesame oil

Mash the beans until smooth. Add all the other ingredients, and just enough water to moisten so the mixture is stiff and not too sticky. Shape into slightly flattened patties. Bake on an oiled cookie sheet at 375° for 25 minutes, or until the top is a little crispy.

Serve with Sesame Gravy.

Sesame Gravy

1 c. water
1 heaping T. kuzu
3 T. sesame seeds
2-3 tsp. tamari soy sauce

Roast the seeds by stirring in a skillet over medium heat until they smell nutty and crumble easily between thumb and forefinger. Grind into a butter in the blender or suribachi. Dissolve kuzu in cool water, then combine all ingredients and heat. Stir until it thickens.

Millet Burgers

3 c. cooked millet*
1 carrot, grated fine
1 onion, minced
1 clove garlic, minced
1 tsp. sesame oil

¼ c. whole grain breadcrumbs
3 T. roasted sesame seeds
1 T. tamari soy sauce
¼ tsp. thyme or marjoram
½ tsp. sage, rubbed
¼ c. fresh minced parsley

* 1 c. millet makes
   3 c. cooked...see
   p. 21 for directions

Here's a terrific way to introduce millet to kids and guests.

Lightly saute carrot, garlic and onion in oil. Cover and cook on low heat 5 minutes. Mix in a large bowl with other ingredients. Shape into 6 or 8 burgers. If too crumbly, add a little water til they hold together well. Bake on an oiled cookie sheet at 375° for 40 minutes, or until crisp on the surface. Or, to save time, press into a shallow baking dish and make Millet Loaf.

Serve burgers with all the trimmings... Tofu Mayo, mustard, pickles, etc.... on whole wheat buns or pita. Enjoy the loaf with a hearty Black Bean or rich Sesame Gravy.

Tofu Mayo

8 oz. tofu
¼ c. water
2 tsp. sesame or olive oil
1 T. lemon juice
1 T. brown rice vinegar
1 T. mellow white miso
optional sprinkle of dill

Slice tofu and steam for just 3 minutes. Blend all ingredients until smooth and creamy. Keeps refrigerated for 2-3 days (if it separates, just re-blend).

Black Bean Gravy

1 c. cooked Gingered Black
   Beans (see p. 27)
water
1 green onion
1 tsp. mirin
1-2 tsp. tamari soy sauce

So easy and delicious! Heat beans. Stir and add just enough water to make a velvety smooth, pourable gravy. Add thin-sliced green onion, mirin, and tamari to taste. Simmer briefly to blend flavors.

Surprisingly Italian

Mama Mia, what's next? Spaghetti with no tomatoes...pizza with tofu? These low-stress Italian dishes are a real treat for people who want to avoid the nightshade vegetables or high-fat cheeses.

Marinara Spaghetti Sauce

Basic Sauce

6 carrots & 1 small beet
Or, 6 c. butternut squash, diced
1 large onion, quartered
1 stalk celery, sliced
1 bay leaf
1½ c. water

The Flavor & Fun

3-4 cloves garlic
1 onion, minced
1-2 tsp. olive or sesame oil
1 tsp. basil or thyme
1 tsp. oregano
¼ c. parsley, minced
2 T. miso or tamari soy sauce
2 heaping T. kuzu, dissolved
in ½ c. cool water

For meaty texture, add:
1 c. minced seitan
or 1 c. sauteed mushrooms

Use carrots and beet for a red sauce. For a delicate, sweeter orange sauce, try squash.

Place Basic Sauce ingredients in a pressure cooker. Bring to pressure, then simmer 20 minutes. Or, pot-boil 30 minutes. Puree in blender. Add water, if needed, for tomato sauce texture.

Saute garlic, onion and herbs for 5 minutes. Add optional seitan or mushrooms and saute 10 minutes more. Next, add sauce and bring to a boil. Then, cover and simmer 10 minutes to blend flavors. Season with miso or tamari. Add kuzu, stirring until thick and shiny.

Tofu Ricotta Sauce

2 tsp. olive or sesame oil
2 onions
4 cloves garlic
1# tofu, drained
2-3 T. tamari soy sauce
½ c. water
½ tsp. basil or thyme
½ tsp. oregano
1 T. chopped parsley

Saute onion and garlic in oil. Dice tofu. Add, with tamari, water, and herbs. Cover and simmer 15 minutes. For a creamy/chunky texture, blend half in the blender, and mash the other half. Layer with Marinara Sauce in lasagna, or on pizza. Or, simply serve with fresh cooked pasta.

Tofu Pizza

THE CRUST

2¼ c. whole wheat flour
3/4 c. water
¼ tsp. sea salt
1 tsp. olive oil

Warm the water and dissolve salt. Mix with
oil, then stir into flour and form into a dough.
Knead 300 times or until smooth. Let sit several
hours, in a warm place, covered with damp towels.
Roll into two 12" crusts or one cookie-sheet-size
crust. Place on oiled pans, then top as follows:

THE TOPPING

Spread a thick layer of Marinara Sauce, then add
Tofu Ricotta Sauce. Add an optional sprinkle of
parmesan or mozarella, then top with your choice
of the following goodies. Bake at 375° for 30-
40 minutes, or 'til it bubbles.

mushrooms
green pepper
sliced onions
wheatmeat (seitan)
for a wild idea--add
cooked arame or
hijiki seaweed!

Tofu Lasagna

Make both sauces (Marinana & Tofu Ricotta). Oil a 9 x 13
baking dish and layer sauces with cooked whole wheat lasagna
noodles and choice morsels of mushroom, sauteed tempeh, and/or
steamed, chopped greens. Top with the tofu sauce or a generous
sprinkle of parmesan. Bake at 375°, 30-40 minutes or till it
bubbles.

Festive Salads

Crispy Cabbage-Dill

1/2 small head cabbage
1 bunch watercress
1/2 small carrot
brown rice vinegar
tamari soy sauce
roasted pumpkin seeds , or
sunflower sprouts (optional)
dill

Cut cabbage in small squares, and slice watercress fine. Julienne cut carrots, then dice fine, to make "confetti".

Plunge vegetables in boiling water for 1 to 2 minutes--just long enough to tenderize, but keep crisp and colorful.

Drain and cool in a strainer. Toss with seeds and sprouts, and about 1 tsp. each of vinegar and tamari, to taste. Season liberally with dill.

Delicious with Christmas dinner.

Rice Wedding Salad

4 c. cooked brown rice
½ c. each, lightly steamed:
    carrot
    cauliflower
    green beans
½ c. raw celery
¼ c. minced parsley
½ c. tamari-roasted almonds
½ # shellfish (shrimp or crab)

DRESSING:

2 T. sesame oil
2 T. water
2 T. brown rice vinegar
2 T. lemon juice
1 clove garlic
1 T. tamari soy sauce
½ tsp. basil
1 tsp. oregano

Marry the vegetables by cutting them in friendly, compatible shapes. Combine all ingredients and toss with dressing. Best if it marinates a few hours before serving.

Holiday Feasting

Special Qualities	The Old Way	The New
Hearty & Roasted	ham turkey chicken beef potatoes	loaves with grains, beans & vegetables broiled fish wheatmeat roasted squash or roots roasted nuts & seeds chestnuts

Creamy & Buttered	mashed potatoes
	buttery soups
	white sauce
	
	sour cream &
	mayonnaise
		millet "mashed potatoes"
		oat cream soups
		bechamel sauce with
		   sesame oil or tahini
		tofu dips and salad
		   dressings

Sweet & Glazed	jello salads
	sugared yams
	sugar, honey or
	   lard glazes
		agar agar gels
		baked squash with cinnamon
		barley malt/miso/
		   sesame oil glazes
		kuzu/apple juice glazes

Gravy	meat gravies	brown gravy with mushroom or onion kuzu gravies bean gravies
Decorated	marshmallows food coloring candies	roasted seeds & nuts raisins mandala arrangements of vegetables, casseroles, and salads

Brown Gravy

6 T. whole wheat flour
2 T. sesame oil
1/2 onion, minced fine
or, 6 mushrooms, sliced
2 c. water or vegetable stock
1 tsp. thyme
2 tsp. marjoram
1 - 2 T. tamari soy sauce
½ tsp. minced lemon peel
   (optional)

Roast the flour by stirring in a skillet over medium heat until fragrant, but not browned. In a saucepan, saute onion or mushroom in oil. Add flour, and cook 5 minutes on low heat, stirring occasionally. Briskly stir in water. Add herbs and tamari. Put a flame spreader under the pot, cover, and simmer 20 minutes. Adjust seasoning. For a very smooth gravy, blend briefly.

Millet "Mashed Potatoes"

2 c. millet
1 small cauliflower
(approx. 2 c. flowerettes)
¼ tsp. sea salt
7 c. water
extra water for mashing

Lightly roast millet (see basic millet recipe, p. 21). Bring water to a boil, and add millet, cauliflower and salt. Cover and simmer 25 minutes. Puree in a food mill or food processor, adding a little water if necessary, for a consistency that's surprisingly akin to mashed potatoes!

Mushroom-Seitan* Gravy

2 shiitake mushrooms (dried)
soaked in 1½ c. water
2 pieces seitan*
1½ heaping T. kuzu, dissolved
in ¼ c. cool water
tamari soy sauce to taste

Soak mushrooms 1 hour. Slice (set aside tough stems to use in soup stock). Bring to a boil with soaking water, cover and simmer 15 minutes. Slice seitan in slender strips. Add and simmer 5 minutes more. Dissolve kuzu in cool water. Add and stir until gravy thickens. Flavor with tamari.

*SEITAN....A meaty, flavorful wheat gluten product, high in protein...a great addition to gravy or stuffing.

Savory Stuffing

NATURAL STUFFING INGREDIENTS:

BREADY (Choose 1 or 2)

whole grain breadcubes
dried breadcrumbs
cooked long-grain brown rice
cooked wild rice
couscous
cornbread

SAVORY & HERBY (Choose 3 or more)

onion sauteed in sesame oil
   or, toasted sesame oil
fresh parsley
sage
thyme
marjoram
rosemary
minced lemon peel
miso or tamari soy sauce

NUTTY (Choose 1)

roasted almonds
   "   sunflower seeds
   "   walnuts
   "   pumpkin seeds
steamed chestnuts
pine nuts

MOIST (Choose 2 or more)

vegetable soup stock
lemon juice
simmered leeks
simmered celery
sauteed mushrooms
wheatmeat
water chestnuts

3-STEP SAVORY STUFFING (delectably different every time!)

1]   Choose your ingredients intuitively

2]   Taste as you go, and make it extra moist....
     It will dry out a little when you bake it.

3]   Bake in an oiled, covered casserole at
     350° for 1/2 hour. Keep covered until
     ready to serve.

Evolving Cornbread

My mom used to make the best spoonbread. Buttermilk and
honey, baking soda and yellow cornmeal. I remember she used
to pour boiling water over the cornmeal.

So I started experimenting. A little of this, a little of
that. I think I've made about 30 batches of cornbread,
never the same twice. Lately, they're coming closer than
ever to that elusive, golden, moist, and fragrant memory.

This current edition is wheat-free--for all
my friends who are allergic to wheat--
here's to all our temporary symptoms,
in gratitude for the creative leaps
they lead us to take.

2½ c. boiling water
1 & 3/4 c. cornmeal
1/2 c. barley flour
(or, whole wheat)
1/4 c. rice or oat flour
1½ c. cooked millet
1½ T. sesame oil
¼ tsp. sea salt
½ c. extra water

Roast the cornmeal, stirring in a skillet on
medium heat until it smells sweet. Put the
cornmeal in a bowl and pour boiling water over
it, then let it sit, covered, for 10 minutes.
Roast other flours. Mix everything together,
and add extra water, if needed, for a consistency
that's midway between batter and dough. Oil
a skillet, spread batter. Decorate with a
few pumpkin seeds. Bake at 375° for 45 minutes.

Delicious with carrot butter or
unsweetened apple butter.

10 Practical Guidelines

Inside yourself, there's a still, small voice
ready to guide you on your healing path.

Listen carefully to your body and mind and you will
hear it speak, in a thousand, different ways. "Yes,
this feels right," it murmurs...."Keep going, you're
getting close." At other times it clearly protests,
"No, Stop! You're getting off track."

Seven years ago, when I first started to cook macro-
biotically, I gobbled up every available book on the
subject. I found many contradictions. But this intrigued
me. I felt compelled to search for my own truth, invent
my own recipes, write my own rules. Then, the essence
of macrobiotics came alive for me and my friends.

Everything changes. We are all different. Together,
we are influenced by powerful forces as they ebb and flow
throughout the universe. Conscious whole foods cooking can
help us balance these forces in our bodies and our lives--
giving us the strength, calmness and clarity of mind
to aim for world peace.

Right now, Earth is changing fast. Use the following
guidelines to help you keep pace. They represent the
collective wisdom of many people who have intuitively
adapted a macrobiotic diet to their changing needs:

* TO RECOVER FROM MINOR ILLNESS
* TO LOSE WEIGHT
* TO MAINTAIN WEIGHT
* TO CLEANSE AND REBUILD
* TO NOURISH GROWING KIDS

Then let us know what happens. Your discoveries
are an important part of the whole.

To Recover From Minor Illness

Feeling fatigued? Have a sore throat, sniffles, cough, headache, stomach upset or mild fever? Maybe you're coming down with a bug.

But remember, bugs are only a tiny part of the Big Picture. You have the power to help change the internal conditions that make you susceptible to bugs. And you can start today by experimenting with one important guideline: Eat Simply.

The simple foods listed below will help to cleanse your intestines and alkalanize your blood (most viruses thrive in stagnant bowel and acid-blood conditions created when we habitually eat too much fat, sugar, and protein).

If possible, ask a friend to cook for you. Rest. Let go of routine mealtimes. And trust your appetite, even if it's small.

Eat when you're hungry. Eat slowly....until you feel soothed. But stop short of familiar feelings of fullness. Leave room to breathe in healing oxygen, and thank the trees for providing it. (Go out and hug a tree, if you feel up to it!)

While you digest your simple meal, sit back and relax. Use the following Self-Healing Exercises to help you listen inside, and activate your inner, creative healing resources. You may be surprised how quickly the bugs decide to leave.

Eat Simply

Easy Vegetable Soup with Miso or Tamari

Whole Cooked Grains

Vegetable & Sea Vegetable Side Dishes

Optional Beans (small quantities)

Cooked Fruits (only if your symptoms are contractive. See p. 35.

Appropriate Tea & Home Remedies (see the Healing Foods Glossary, p. 195)

And Minimize:

dairy & animal foods
fat (nuts, oil, seeds, etc.)
sweet & spices
processed foods
bread & flour products
caffeine & alcohol
tropical fruit
nightshade veggies
(potato, tomato, peppers and eggplant)

Self-Healing Exercises

Visualize

1] Visualize healing colors streaming through your blood...relaxing your body and mind. Let them soothe swollen membranes, break up congestion, carry away accumulations. Breathe deep.

Gradually, let the colors spread. Surround yourself with them. Bathe in their light. Imagine that right now they are lighting up dark areas in your life....in your home and work environment. What changes?

See yourself healed. In your mind's eye, reach out and touch a friend with your love. What feels different?

Then, rest, relax even deeper....Feel healing energy pulse through your whole body, renewing every cell. Breathe......

Draw

2] Draw a picture of how you feel. Include aches and pains (scribble!), also any subtle clues that you're getting better. Use colors and shapes that intuitively appeal to you. If one picture isn't enough, make another....and another....until you feel complete.

Write

3] Write a story, poem, or stream-of-consciousness word association about an ideal day, 5 years from now. Include lots of detail. Thank your symptoms for slowing you down....to dream big dreams.

Share

4] Finally, tell a friend or family member your healing insights. Show them your pictures. Read them your story. Good medicine stories grow even more potent when they're shared.

To Lose Weight Naturally

In most traditional societies, folks were seldom overweight. They honored the sacred spirit in every food. Cooked natural whole foods in season. And got plenty of exercise from the rigorous, year-round activity required for self-reliant living.

By contrast, most Americans suffer from the lack of a truly nourishing daily rhythm. And most of us are overweight.

We eat when we're not hungry. Many of us compulsively overeat, in an attempt to comfort and insulate ourselves from the stresses of modern life. We eat alone. Filling up on fast foods high in fat, sugar, salt, and chemicals. Dieting for as long as we can stand it. Then filling up again when loneliness, frustration, or anxiety hit home.

Not everyone who is overweight overeats. Years of sedentary living, combined with chronic dieting on devitalized, chemicalized low-cal foods, can toxify our internal organs. Gradually, our metabolism slows down, and even small portions of food start to keep the weight on. So discouraging!

Our national weight problem is much bigger than any of us can face alone. (In the last 20 years, the incidence of obesity in American kids has doubled!).

That's why, in our hometown, my husband Rich and I, decided together with Dr. Stephen Banister, M.D. and his wife Sharon, to co-direct a holistic program for eating disorders and weight manage-ment, called Weight Success.

In this program, we encourage our friends and neighbors to team up and help each other explore the Big Picture of factors contri-buting to weight gain and permanent weight management.

SLIM TRADITIONAL PEOPLES...

celebrated each new season with community fasting, feasting, and dancing. Doesn't that sound like a lot more fun than dieting, bingeing, and exercis-ing at the gym?

Here's what we've discovered.

Lasting weight loss is the natural result of carving out a more truly nourishing lifestyle with each other. A lifestyle with simple, heartfelt values that reflect our common concerns: cooperation, interdependence, neighborliness, renewal of family life, respect for natural cycles, and love for Mother Nature.

Sharing these values creates an atmosphere in which caring relationships flourish. We listen to each other's problems. Reflect the progress we see. And help each other to break free from compulsive daily routines and the eating habits that have compensated for them. Joy bubbles up. Spills over to our family and friends. And the energy that used to be so contained inside is freed up for purposeful, rewarding work.

Looking back now, group members can hardly believe that they used to think just eating the right foods was enough. For some members, the most important factors in keeping the weight off include emotional clearing and spiritual centering. But for others, a flexible balanced natural foods diet has been invaluable in enabling them to feel light, clear, and more at peace in their bodies than ever before.

The following Slimming Diet Guidelines have emerged from their experience. Please let us know how these work for you (we'll value your feedback, for future writing).

But before you rush to turn the page.... slow down and consider one important fact. Rarely does anyone succeed at tackling weight problems all alone. Think a moment. Who could you ask to join you? Reach out, pick up the phone, and lighten up together.

THE ALL-AMERICAN LIFESTYLE YO-YO DIET

1. Work harder

2. Succeed faster

3. Grab more fast food

4. Use that MONEY & TIME you save....to buy & read more books on "How to Reduce Stress"

5. Exercise frantically (or half-heartedly)

6. When this routine starts to weigh you down, DIET!

7. Then, go back to #1 and repeat this cycle, endlessly

Slimming Diet Guidelines

1]   WHOLE GRAIN VARIETY

2]   SENSUOUS VEGGIES & LOCAL FRUITS

3]   LOW-FAT, LIGHT PROTEIN MEALS

4]   SPECIAL, CLEANSING FOODS DAILY

5]   BE IMPERFECT--LOVE YOURSELF WITH TREATS

6]   DARE TO BE YOURSELF--EAT WHAT FITS FOR YOU

1]   <u>WHOLE GRAIN VARIETY</u>

Emphasize digestable, well-chewed grains...brown
rice, millet, barley, quinoa, bulghar, or buckwheat.
For variety, cook rice with wheat, barley, rye or
sweet rice. Fresh corn in season (rub with umeboshi
instead of butter for a tasty surprise). But
minimize oats--they're highest in fat.

2]   <u>SENSUOUS VEGGIES & LOCAL FRUITS</u>

Branch out from salad and steamed veggies, with:
*   creamy, non-dairy vegetable soups
    (cook, then puree in blender)
*   colorful, quick-cooked shredded veggies
*   sweet, baked winter squash
*   rice and veggie salads (w/ lemon, vinegar, tamari)
*   gingery chinese vegetables
*   crunchy & refreshing quick-boiled salads

<u>Fat-Dissolving Vegetables:</u> Eat one or more of these
everyday....radish, turnip, onion, green onion, leek,
shiitake mushroom, or daikon. (See Daikon Weight-Loss
Condiment, p. 196).

<u>Dark Leafy Greens:</u> Eat 'em 2-3 times daily...they're
highly mineralized & great for improving metabolism
(try kale, bok choy, collards, turnip greens, watercress, mustard greens, etc.)

<u>Local Fruits:</u> Enjoy in season, for a treat...apple,
pear, peach, berries, watermelon, etc.....But to curb
a sweet-tooth and minimize weight-producing sugars,
eat less fruit, more vegetables.

3] <u>LOW-FAT, LIGHT PROTEIN MEALS</u>

Minimize meat, eggs, cheese, butter, milk, nuts,
nut butter, & mayo (see <u>Where's The Fat</u>, p. 43)
Adults get plenty of protein from a grain and
veggie diet which includes beans, fish & seeds.
Try these portions: 1/2 c. cooked beans 3-5 times
a week, 2-4 oz. white-meat fish or tofu 1-2 times a
week, and occasional toasted seeds as a snack.

4] <u>SPECIAL CLEANSING FOODS</u>

<u>Sea Vegetables</u>: Small portions daily help to
cleanse your blood, tone intestines & provide
vitamins & minerals to improve metabolism.

<u>Burdock Root</u>: Eat 1-3 times a week, to cleanse
the blood, and help build will power (see p. 196).

<u>Hato Mugi Barley</u>: Want to try something really
different? This tasty, cleansing grain is used
often in Chinese medicine. Eat it 3-4 times a
month, or whenever you feel frustrated, bloated,
or sluggish. Cook with rice or in soups. To order
by mail, see Mt. Ark Co., (<u>Resources</u>, p. 206).

5] <u>BE IMPERFECT--LOVE YOURSELF WITH A TREAT</u>

<u>Need richness</u>? Make a Creamy Tahini Dressing.
Sprinkle cheese on Tofu Lasagna. Or, saute favorite
veggies in a little toasted sesame oil & tamari.

<u>Have a sweet-tooth?</u> Love yourself openly, instead
of sneaking off with chocolate. Make a mini-batch
of Oatmeal Raisin Cookies or Strawberry Couscous
Cake. Be impure. Savor your humanness.

6] <u>DARE TO BE YOURSELF--EAT WHAT FITS FOR YOU</u>

Everybody's different. Do you need to lighten those
thighs and liberate the lover inside you? Give up
peanut butter, and reach for greens & fat-dissolving
veggies. If, in contrast, your friend wants to gain
the will power to pass up sweets and pass exams....
tell her to eat more brown rice, aduki beans, roots,
and homemade treats. Study the following <u>Slim
Rhythms</u> Charts. Help each other discover what fits.

Slim Rhythms...

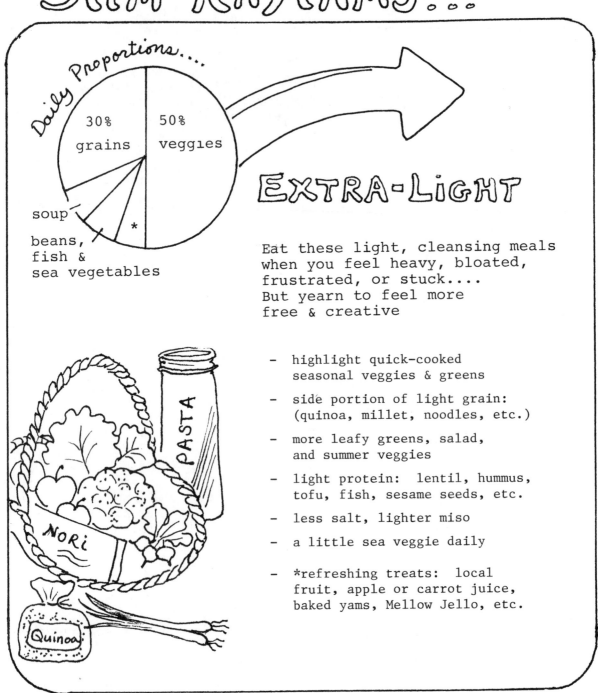

Daily Proportions....

30% grains

50% veggies

soup

beans, fish & sea vegetables

*

EXTRA-LIGHT

Eat these light, cleansing meals when you feel heavy, bloated, frustrated, or stuck....
But yearn to feel more free & creative

- highlight quick-cooked seasonal veggies & greens

- side portion of light grain: (quinoa, millet, noodles, etc.)

- more leafy greens, salad, and summer veggies

- light protein: lentil, hummus, tofu, fish, sesame seeds, etc.

- less salt, lighter miso

- a little sea veggie daily

- *refreshing treats: local fruit, apple or carrot juice, baked yams, Mellow Jello, etc.

PASTA

NORi

Quinoa

Because your appetite naturally fluctuates with changing moods, it's important to vary your weight-loss diet, according to how you feel each day. Listen to your body. Learn to trust the subtle cues it give you. Also, pay attention to Nature's cycles....

MORE GROUNDED

Eat these low-fat, grounding meals when you feel scattered, weak, or overwhelmed....
or anytime you need more will power & stamina

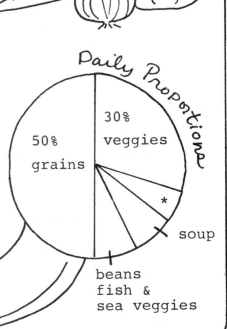

- highlight whole grains
  (millet, brown rice, etc.)

- side portion of veggies
  (mostly cooked, sometimes raw)

- more roots, sturdy greens,
  and winter squash

- hearty protein: aduki or black
  beans, fish, pumpkin seeds, etc.

- mildly salty, darker miso

- a little sea veggie daily

- *grounding treats: baked squash,
  Creamy Rice Pudding, Mochi,
  Soothy Applesauce, etc.

Daily Proportions

50% grains

30% veggies

*

soup

beans
fish &
sea veggies

...The new and full moon, menstruation and ovulation, hot and cold weather, all affect moods and appetite, too. Start to notice what your body needs during each of these cycles, to stay in balance. Which of these two types of meals most fits for you, today?

To Regain Weight

Fed up with people telling you that you are too thin? Feeling helpless to know how to gain back your comfort zone?

I can empathize. I have a fast-burning metabolism and a tall, light build-- and in times of stress and illness I can lose weight too quickly! I know what it takes to recover from debilitating weight loss--a full plate of nourishing resources for the body, mind and spirit.

At the core, chronic underweight is an invitation to care for yourself better than you ever thought possible.

Get massages to improve circulation. Bring living plants into your house to oxygenate your environment. Exercise gently--yoga, tai chi, or qi gong all offer excellent ways to relax, energize and harmonize your body systems, improving impaired digestive functions.

Seek counsel from nutritionally-informed health professionals. Holistic medical doctors, acupuncturists, herbalists, chiropractors, homeopathic and naturo- pathic physicians each have unique perspectives on the possible causes (see sidebar) and treatment of malabsorp- tion and low weight.

Emotional causes of your inability to gain weight may include current stress, as well as past trauma or losses. Anything that triggers the body/mind's memory of traumatic events can stimulate your fight-flight-or-freeze response-- shutting down digestion and hampering the immune system.

Learning how to repattern your responses to stress can help you regain vitality and stabilize weight more quickly.

CAUSES OF LOW WEIGHT
CAN INCLUDE:

allergies (to foods
  or environment)
dehydration
eating disorders
endocrine imbalance
genetic body type
parasites
serious illness
toxins

UNDERLYING
MISTAKEN BELIEFS
MAY INCLUDE:

"I'm a failure."
"I have to be in control."
"I'm not enough."
"I'm not lovable."

One effective way to identify and clear up internal stressors that can interfere with nutrient absorption is a biofeedback method called BodyTalk (see Resources, p. 206).

For streamlined stress relief,
I highly recommend two pioneering
biofeedback methods designed to
clear up self-limiting patterns in
the body/mind--Healing From the
Body Level Up, and BodyTalk (see
Resources, p. 206).

In your search for nourishing food
choices, ask your body for clues
about what it needs. For example,
read the sidebar and notice how
your body responds. When do you
feel your mouth water, take a deeper
breath, or lick your lips? Watch
for these body cues when you open the
fridge, or stroll the grocery aisle.

Next, take a moment to imagine how
each potential food choice will feel
in your belly a few hours after you
eat. Do some foods promise excitement, but leave you cold or dry?
Which ones will create warmth, energy,
comfort or relaxation hours from now?

Choose to eat what gives your
body the most pleasurable sensations deep inside, long after you
taste and chew. This daily
practice in awareness can awaken your
intuitive attraction to the foods
that will fortify and sustain you.

"Do you ever wonder what you are eating?
Beyond the fiber, the fat, the taste,
the crunch? We are eating life itself.
Powerful forces stream down to us from
the cosmos, and rise up from the earth.
We draw our nourishment...from the
life energy and spirit within the food."

— Anne Scott
Serving Fire

TO REGAIN WEIGHT*
Listen to your body
and consider these choices:

Feel cold or vulnerable?

Oatmeal
Pressure-cooked grains--
   rice, sweet rice, millet
Buckwheat soba noodles
Mochi
Quinoa
Aduki or black beans, lentil
   garbanzo or pinto beans
Baked casseroles
Tempeh
Seitan (wheat gluten)
Hearty soups
Sturdy veggies: carrot, onion
   parsnip, turnip, broccoli
   collards, burdock, rutabaga
Sweet squashes
Hijiki, arame, kombu, wakame
Fish or seafood
Naturally-raised fowl
Whole grain breads
Toasted seeds or nuts
Cooked local fruits
Grain-sweetened desserts

Feel tense or dry?

Rice cream
Bulghar or couscous
Fresh corn
Brown basmati rice
Stir-fried vegetables
Noodles
Tofu
Hummus
Fish
Lentils, split peas
Uplifting veggies:
   steamed leafy greens
   peas, green beans
   cauliflower, sprouts
   summer squash, cukes
   scallions, watercress
Nori sushi
Sensuous fruit desserts
Fresh local fruit

*Invite your intuition to
 guide you to more options

To Cleanse and Rebuild

Feeling low energy, overwhelmed, or irritable?
Trying to cope by eating unhealthy snacks?
Time to pause and take positive steps to renew
yourself, before you get sick.

Start by listening closely to recurring signals
from your body and moods. These are nature's way
of telling you when stressed internal organs need
cleansing and rebuilding.

The cues listed below are just a few of thousands
used by traditional Oriental healers to diagnose
the internal imbalances that create illness.

Study this chart and check the body/mood cues you
notice most often. Then read the next 5 pages to
learn how to start a cleanse and choose foods most
appropriate for your needs.

Organ Stress Checklist

ORGANS*	✓ MOOD SIGNALS	✓ BODY CUES
SPLEEN-PANCREAS/ STOMACH	feel scattered anxious, worried overly sensitive big mood swings	erratic energy levels bingeing on sweets belching, upset stomach low resistance to infections
LUNGS/ LARGE INTESTINES	sad or depressed nostalgic stuck weary	fatigue stuffy sinuses, phlegm pale complexion gas, constipation, diarrhea
KIDNEYS/ BLADDER	overwhelmed confused afraid insecure	frequent, pale urine or scant, dark urine lower back ache low sexual energy bags under the eyes often feel cold
LIVER/ GALL BLADDER	impatient frustrated angry blocked creativity	headaches often overeat eyes irritated or bloodshot oily or dry skin restless from 11PM to 2 AM
HEART/ SMALL INTESTINES	over-excitable can't relax chronic tension workaholic	chest aching or tense backache between shoulders high blood pressure red complexion

* In Oriental medicine, each organ pair listed above has complementary,
balancing functions (see Muramoto, Healing Ourselves).

How To Start A Cleanse

1] Right Timing

First, sit quietly and ask yourself: "Is this
a good time to start a cleanse?" Don't try
for a quick answer. Let images float to mind.
Be alert for unusual body sensations.

You may, for example, get that same squeamish
feeling you sometimes have when you find the
garbage overflowing under the sink, or the
unbalanced bank statements in your desk drawer.
If so, you know it's time to cleanse! But if,
on the other hand, your shoulders sag at the
weighty thought of tackling one more challenge,
better to wait. Get on with priority business.
Invite your body to let you know when it's
ready to lighten up inside. And promise you'll
listen. Cooperating with your inner sense of
timing makes it much easier to start and follow
through with the discipline of a cleanse.

2] Start Simply

For 1-3 days, eat light, bland meals. Low
in fat, sweet, salt, spices, and protein.
Think clean tasting. Chew very well.
And keep menus easy:

Soup
Cooked whole grain (not bread or cereal)
Steamed, boiled or raw veggies
Spring water and/or mild tea

Between meals, have steamed veggie snacks,
optional local fruits, or occasional fresh
juices (apple, vegetable or wheat grass).

Take a walk before and/or after your meals,
to stimulate circulation and encourage
discharge of toxins.

Also, before and after eating, take time to
relax. Listen to music. Be quiet in nature.
Spend time with a nourishing friend.
Stretch. Dance. Help your body let go.

Cleaning With The Seasons

ORGANS	GOOD SEASON TO CLEANSE	FOODS THAT STRESS THESE ORGANS	BENEFICIAL FOODS*
Spleen-Pancreas/ Stomach	LATE SUMMER (and, during every change of season)	sugar & honey high-fat foods tropical fruit juices MSG, food additives	millet & sweet vegetables round, compact veggies--turnip, cabbage, onion, rutabaga, pumpkin, etc. arame, kombu, miso soup local sweet fruit (occas.)
Lungs/ Large Intestines	FALL	white flour yeasted breads high-fat foods sugar & honey antibiotics food color, additives	brown rice & dark leafy greens roots, winter squash onion, leek, ginger, garlic hijiki, wakame, miso soup apples, pears (occas.)
Kidneys/ Bladder	WINTER	ice cold food & drink milk and dairy foods too much raw food sugar & honey over-salting	brown rice, buckwheat, aduki beans sturdy greens, roots, winter squash kombu, hijiki, arame, miso soup watermelon extract (for contracted kidneys) or, in season, watermelon, berries (occas.)
Liver/ Gall Bladder	SPRING	overeating--especially eggs, meat, cheese, & ice cream alcohol & drugs chemicalized foods coffee & chocolate sugar & honey	barley, quinoa, wheat, rye daikon & spring greens broccoli, cabbage, cauliflower, parsley wakame, sea palm umeboshi, lemon, sauerkraut (occas.)
Heart/ Small Intestines	SUMMER	all of the above	corn, quinoa, pot-boiled brown rice bitter greens & summer veggies sea palm, nori strawberries & other local fruit (occas.)

*It's OK to eat these foods out of season, if your body
 signals the need. Emphasize but don't limit yourself to
 these cleansing foods. Trust your intuition to guide you.

3] <u>Take Care of Your Body</u>

In the morning, to help circulate lymph and expel toxins, dry skin brush your whole body.

In the evening, scrub your body with a hot, wet washcloth until the skin gets red (especially legs and feet). Dry vigorously.

Exchange back or foot rubs with a friend.

4] <u>After 3 Days</u>

If you crave sweets, or your energy lags, add protein to your meals, with toasted seeds, aduki beans, lentils, tempeh, etc.

If you crave oily/salty foods, have Sesame Salt or Sunflower Sea Palm Crunch with your meal. Also, try veggies sauteed in a few drops of toasted sesame oil and soy sauce.

Be quiet with your body every day. Listen for changes. If you feel great, keep going! Trust your intuition to tell you when to ease back towards social eating.

5] <u>Be Kind To Yourself</u>

Don't expect to do it perfect. Plan to indulge in a few treats, even in the midst of cleansing. Celebrate your humanness.

6] <u>Cleanse With The Seasons</u>

Just like your car needs a regular oil change, your body needs regular cleansing to run smoothly.

Oriental healers know that in every season two inter-related organs get stimulated to cleanse and rebuild. Your food choices can either block this natural cleansing cycle, or help it flow. See the preceding chart, (based on the 5 Element Theory from traditional Chinese medicine) to fine-tune your diet for specific organs and seasons.

BAGS UNDER YOUR EYES? Feel overwhelmed, and easily chilled (especially in winter)? Signs of kidney stress. Eat more aduki beans, roots, and sturdy greens. Cut down on raw foods and ice cold drinks.

To learn more body/mood cues like these, see <u>The Book of Oriental Diagnosis: How To See Your Health</u>, by Kushi.

A cleansing diet
helps restore beneficial
intestinal bacteria
destoyed by:

_____

sugar
meat
dairy
fatty foods
birth control pills
antibiotics

INTESTINAL CLEANSING

Almost everybody in America could use several weeks on a good, cleansing diet designed to renew the colon. Here's why.

Most of us grew up eating plenty of dairy, meat and other high-fat foods, sugar, and chemicals. Many of us have taken frequent doses of antibiotics or birth control pills.

These foods and drugs, when routinely consumed, can destroy beneficial, aerobic bacteria in the intestines, which help to digest our food.

A healthy gut has millions of these friendly bacteria. They thrive on grains and vegetables, and produce B vitamins to help us cope with stress. But if we eat too much sugar, meat, etc., they die off. Unfriendly, anaerobic bacteria take their place, inhibiting proper digestion.

The result? Foods stagnate and putrify inside us, especially if there's no fiber to keep things moving. Pockets of hard fecal matter line the colon walls. Abdominal muscles become too tense or loose (either way, losing their ability to push). Constipation, loose stools, unpleasant gas and odors become the norm.

Recently, with the increasing use of antibiotics, many research doctors report that the candida bacteria, which originally overgrows in the intestines, can apparently spread throughout the body, causing a wide variety of seemingly unrelated symptoms: headaches, confusion, bloating, food allergies, gas, and more (see William Crook, The Yeast Connection).

A cleansing diet can do much to reverse these symptoms, re-establish beneficial bacteria, and encourage new muscle tone in the colon. See the next page, for colon cleansing guidelines.

Gentle, Colon Cleanse Guidelines

EASE IN	For 3-7 days, take a break from protein, fat and sweet. Eat soups, grains, and seasonal veggies.
SOUP	Warm soup relaxes the intestines. Have some every day, and include cleansing sea vegetables.
GRAINS & VEGGIES	Emphasize whole-cooked grains (brown rice, millet, quinoa, etc.), and organically grown veggies.... especially quick-cooked leafy greens and fat-dissolvers, such as kale, chinese cabbage, daikon and scallion. (Choose proportions of grain to veggies according to your moods--see Slim Rhythms, pp. 180-181.)
EAT GENTLY	Chew everything well. De-stress your colon by avoiding most flour products and hard, dry foods (rice cakes, popcorn). For easily digested variety, have noodles, rice cream, or a slice of steamed unyeasted bread.
PROTEIN	After 3-7 days, include protein as needed for warmth and strength...aduki, lentil, garbanzo, toasted seeds.
SIMPLIFY	Eat 2 meals, unless you're hungry for three. Reduce salt and spices. Avoid mucus-forming foods: nuts, oil, tofu, and dairy foods. Season with a little ginger, garlic, umeboshi, caraway seeds, fennel, dill or thyme.
TEA JUICE & FRUIT	Drink spring water and mild teas (clover, nettles, twig, roasted barley, etc.). For treats enjoy local fruit, apple or vegetable juice, or Mellow Jello.
RENEW FLORA	To renew intestinal flora, have small amounts of miso or tamari in soup, and a little daikon pickle or sauerkraut after supper. (If, however, these cause candida flare-up, switch to non-fat yogurt, acidophilous or megadophilous).
KEEP IT MOVING	Walk daily (or dance and stretch!). Gentle, rhythmic movement stimulates colon action.

To increase circulation and expel toxins, apply ginger compress on belly 2-4 times a week (see p. 198).

For the most thorough cleanse, continue to eat simply for several weeks, while taking intestinal herbs and psyllium husks, marketed by Holistic Horizons. (For details on these herbal aids, see The Colon Health Handbook, by Robert Gray).

To Nourish Growing Kids

Bless all of you who are raising conscious kids.
I love to meet children who care how food affects
their bodies, moods, and the quality of life on Earth.
(Kids who know, for example, that organic farmers help
renew the soil, clean the air, purify the water, and bring
back the wildlife that chemicals have nearly destroyed).

Thanks for having the guts to experiment with your
family's diet. Thanks too, for reaching out to like-
spirited parents. When you take a cooking class with
a friend, or plan a healthy potluck in the park, you are
teaching kids we can have fun, solving problems together.

Kids do have special nutrition needs. The responsibility
of sensing these needs is awesome. Recent research with
macrobiotic parents who unknowingly ate meals too low in
Vitamin B-12 shows us just how informed and flexible we
must be (see B-12 Facts on the next page).

Use the following guidelines to help your child make
wise food choices. Research and stay open to current
nutrition facts. Get feedback from friends and health
professionals. But most important, listen to your hunches.
Your own observations can tell you whether gradual or
quick action is needed, to create balance in your
child's health.

Children's Nutrition

Compared to adults, most kids age 3-16* need:

MORE PROTEIN	Beans, seeds, tofu, nuts, seitan (wheat gluten), fish
LESS SALT	None for infants, gradually increase with age
MORE FUN FOOD	See p. 192, and make time to play!
LIGHTER COOKING	Quick-cooked veggies, noodles, salad, fruit jello, etc.
GRAIN VARIETY	Less heavy grain, more pasta, cereals & fun breads
YUMMY SWEET VEGGIES	Corn, snow peas, sweet roots & squash (see p. 56)
SALADS & FRUIT	More frequently than adults--emphasize seasonal foods
GREEN POWER!	"Who my kid eat these?" See p. 192 for clever ways to conceal greens & sea veggies (high in calcium & iron).
AMPLE VIT. B-12	See the following B-12 Facts

* For pregnancy & baby foods, see Macrobiotic Pregnancy, and Macrobiotic Family
  Favorites, both by Esko & Kushi (& keep in mind the following B-12 Facts....).

B-12 FACTS

How can we give our kids the very best start in life? This question has motivated parents around the world to learn the art of macrobiotic cooking.

With dismay, many macrobiotic parents in Boston and Holland discovered--through two studies published in 1988--that their infants and toddlers were deficient in Vitamin B-12.*

In planning healthy meals, they had relied on research that claimed seaweed, miso, tempeh and other fermented foods had ample B-12. But this research has now proven faulty. (See sidebar).

Only small amounts of B-12 are needed, for healthy cell development--but those small doses are crucial for pregnant and nursing moms and toddlers. B-12 deficiency weakens red blood cells. Severe symptoms in infants can include lethargy, paleness, vomiting, loss of appetite, and slowed growth. Children in both studies (whose symptoms ranged from mild to serious) improved markedly with increased B-12 in their diets.

But before you rush to buy chicken and milk, folks, consider more subtle facts, too. Environmental toxins, psychological stress, and your past diet can all influence B-12 assimilation. Bacteria which produce B-12 live all around you in nature (they've been found on organic produce and in healthy intestines). Animal foods are the richest known B-12 source. However, fish or supplements may be your best choice--to avoid the health risks of dairy, eggs, and meat.

Kids change every day. Do yours have a spark in their eyes? Vigor in their limbs? Curiosity and adventure in their play? If not, they may need more B-12. Be observant. Cook flexibly, to nurture their joyful strength. Mother Earth will thank you.

---

* For complete details on this research, see East West, May 1988, and Macromuse, April/May, 1988.

Sources of Vit. B-12:

* fish & seafood
* eggs & dairy
* poultry & meat
* possibly nori, kombu & hijiki (research not conclusive)

B-12 Guidelines

* Eat a widely varied Self-Healing Diet (see p. 18). For ample B-12, add small amounts of fish or seafood, 2-3 times a week, (or other animal foods, if craved).

* To aid B-12 absorption, tone the intestines-- with daily fresh-cooked veggies, sea veggies, and small amounts of fermented foods.

* For vegetarian B-12, take supplements. (Try Twin Lab's child-size lozenges).

Fun Food

Put a noodle
in it
Roll it up
Give it a funny name.

Decorate it
Cut it in fun shapes
Blend it smooth
and creamy.

Mix it half & half
with an old favorite
(scramble tofu
with eggs...mix
amasake with milk
on morning cereal).

Most fun of all...
invite a friend
to do it
with you!

SNACKS FOR LITTLE PEOPLE

carrot sticks
raw sugar peas
toasted nori
steamed winter squash
corn on the cob
Sesame Rice Balls
rice cakes or
whole grain bread
with Carrot Butter,
Sesame Squash Butter,
occasional almond butter,
or tahini & apple butter
apple juice & rice shakes
carrot juice popsicles
local organic fruit
puffed cereals with amasake
popcorn
toasted seeds or almonds
Mellow Jello
Oatmeal-Raisin Cookies

Making Changes Fun

Start Simply

Whether you're weaning baby or
introducing big kids to whole foods,
start simply, with grains. Soft-
cooked for infants. Variety for older
kids...brown rice, oatmeal, millet,
noodles, toast, polenta, waffles,
mochi, rice cakes, corn tortillas.
They're nutritious, easy-to-cook,
and most kids love 'em!

Share Decisions

Ask your kids' help deciding which
veggies to add to rice salad tonight...
or which beans to soak for soup tomorrow. Send young detectives hunting in
the store for cereal and bread with
no sugar, honey, or preservatives.

Gradually Re-Green

Dark leafy greens can be appealing to
kids when chopped very fine & added to:

* Colorful Shredded Veggies
* Lentil Noodle Soup
* Noodle Salad (steam greens first)
* Burrito or Tacos   "   "
* Hummus & Pita Sandwiches   "
* Lasagna

For Added Ocean Power

1] Cook kombu with rice (then remove
   it--the minerals get into the rice).

2] Cook kombu with beans--it dissolves.

3] Simmer kombu with carrots, parsnips,
   turnips or daikon--makes 'em tender,
   sweet & mineralized.

4] Add wakame (cut small) to Marinara
   Spaghetti Sauce (cook with the
   carrots--see p. 166).

5] Use 1 tsp. kelp powder to fortify
   cookies or cornbread.

6] Sprinkle Sea Palm Crunch (p. 127)
   on Sesame Smother (p. 72).

Kid Food Projects

Make Friends with a Veggie

At the grocery, find a veggie you've never tasted before. Bring it home. Sit quietly and imagine where it grew. Did bugs tickle it? Angels help it grow? Draw what you see. Then, ask mom or dad to help you cook it! Here's some ideas:

* Slice, steam & eat it on toast with tahini

* Put it in salad, with Tofu Dressing

* Stir-fry it with other colorful veggies

FOOD & MOOD

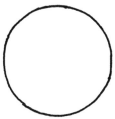

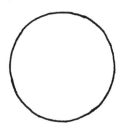

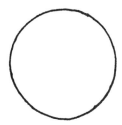

Color in these faces....

Notice when different foods make you feel like each face.

List those foods here.

I feel real excited & jumpy!	I feel very calm, & strong	I feel mean & angry
_____	_____	_____
_____	_____	_____
_____	_____	_____

FAMILY GRAFFITI

Everybody has a right to say "Yuck" to some foods and kitchen chores. Here's how to do it, and make folks chuckle, too. Tape a big piece of paper on the fridge. Ask each family member to draw a cartoon of the food they think is yuckiest. Agree that everybody will draw more cartoons here (instead of your usual ways of bugging each other about food & dishes). Yes, Mom...you too. How 'bout drawing a cartoon of Mr. Speedo Eater?

Ginger-Carrot Breakfast Cookies

CREATIVE COOKING is the art of pairing unexpected combinations to achieve winning flavors, textures, and forms that fulfill a heartfelt need....

Unsweetened cookies for breakfast? Try em!....
They're reminiscent of muffins & sweetrolls, minus the sugar-crash. Many thanks to my 9 year old friend Johnny for the inspiration of ginger!

3/4 c. rolled oats
½ c. oat flour
¼ c. brown rice or barley flour
2 c. cooked millet
1 & ½ T. corn oil
1 c. fine-shredded carrot
1 tsp. vanilla
1 tsp. finely grated ginger
¼ tsp. sea salt
1 T. poppy seeds or sunflower seeds
½ c. water (approx.)

Lightly roast oats & flours by stirring over medium heat in a skillet, until toasty smelling but not browned. Mix all ingredients & add just enough water for a moist, pliable but not mushy dough. Shape into cookies on an oiled baking sheet. Bake at 350° for 30 min.

P.S. This batter makes great muffins, too!... fill tins full, round the tops with a spoon, & bake at 350° for 45 minutes.

Healing Foods Glossary

Well, friends.....
You've had the beef,
the mashed potatoes,
gravy,
and dessert
of Self-Healing.....

Here's the nightcap and seltzer!

Everyone needs an extra boost, on occasion, to
get back in balance.

The following special foods and home remedies
from traditional Oriental folk medicine
may just fill the bill.

Look here when you have an upset tummy,
are coming down with a cold, your back aches,
or you're feeling run down and blah.

Thanks to generations of wise old grannies,
philosophers and physicians,
for passing on these Self-Healing Secrets.

* * * * * *

Of course, not all of these foods
are right for everybody. Consult your intuition.

Keep your senses alert. Taste to understand
How the universe works.

Ultimately,
That's what's healing.

HEALING FOOD	DESCRIPTION & USE:	TRADITIONAL BENEFITS:

BURDOCK

Long, brown root with a savory-sweet flavor. Easy to grow (see Seed Catague addresses, p. 205). Buy fresh in Japanese markets (it keeps for several weeks, well-wrapped and refrigerated). Or, dried as a tea, in health food stores.

Cook like carrots: in soup, stew, or saute as a side dish (approximately 2" per serving). For Tea: simmer 1 tsp. in 1 c. water for 10 minutes.

Cleanses the blood

Tones & strengthens intestines

Improves mental clarity

Alkalanizing and highly mineralized, an excellent booster food when you feel run down from a cold or flu.

Eat often to help reduce sweet cravings

CARROT EXTRACT

Thick, concentrated syrup made from organic carrots. Add 1/8 tsp. to 1/2 cup kukicha twig tea or boiling water.

Tones & vitalizes spleen,

pancreas, liver, and

lymphatic system.

DAIKON

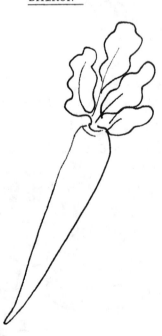

Long, white radish. Sharp taste when raw, but mellow, clean taste when cooked until tender.

In daily cooking: add to soups, stir-fry, steam, or bake with other roots.

Weight-loss condiment: Grate 1 T. raw daikon and sprinkle with a few drops tamari soy sauce. Serve with grain-based meals, 3-5 times a week.... a zingy fat-dissolver.

To reduce fever: Mix 1/2 c. grated daikon with 1-2 tsp. tamari soy sauce and 1/4 tsp. grated ginger. Pour hot twig tea over the mixture. Drink hot, go to bed and rest.

For itching: rub a slice of raw daikon on bites & rashes.

Dissolves excess fat & mucus

Facilitates weight-loss

Reduces fever (in tea)

Relieves itching of bites and rashes (external)

HEALING FOOD	DESCRIPTION & USE:	TRADITIONAL BENEFITS:

DAIKON LEAVES HIP BATH

Brown, brittle-dry leaves from the daikon plant (dry your own, in a shady, aired location).

For women's healing hip bath: Bring 1-2 gallons water to a boil with a big handful of leaves (30-40). Simmer 15 minutes--until water turns brown--then, strain and add to hip-height hot bath, with 1 c. sea salt. Wrap your upper body in a towel and sit in bath for 10 minutes or until perspiring. Douche afterwards with a mix of 1 qt. twig tea, 1/2 lemon squeezed, and pinch sea salt. Then, rest and visualize healing circulation all through your pelvis. Repeat up to 10 days, as needed.

Increases circulation

Draws toxins from vagina and uterus, to help heal infections, cysts, and tumors and renew sexual energy.

NOTE: Do not use if you have high blood pressure, use ginger compress instead.

DANDELION EXTRACT

(also called Yansen)

Thick concentrate made from wild dandelion root, a hardy herb that grows worldwide. Dissolve 1/8-1/4 tsp. in 1/2 c. hot water, twig tea, or roasted barley tea.

Strengthens the heart,

kidneys, liver,

and intestines.

GINGER

Golden, fibrous root with a pungent aroma and spicy, mildly hot taste. Available at most grocers.

For stimulating variety: add finely grated ginger to soups, pilaf, salad dressings, or Chinese vegetables.

For delayed menstruation: Make ginger tea, gently heating two 1/4" crosscut slices of ginger in 1 c. water for 10 minutes (don't boil). Drink 1/2 c. twice daily for no more than 2 days.

Stimulates sluggish intestines

Promotes circulation

Promotes blood flow in delayed menstruation

(also, see Ginger Compress, and Ginger Spine-Rub on the next page....)

HEALING FOOD	DESCRIPTION & USE:	TRADITIONAL BENEFITS:

GINGER COMPRESS

For aches & pains: Grate enough ginger to make a golfball-size ball, and tie in a cheesecloth. Squeeze juice into a gallon of water. Add ginger ball and heat water, but don't boil. Dip a handtowel in water (holding both ends dry), and wring out. Cool briefly, then place on skin. Cover with dry towels to retain heat. Replace every 3-4 min. Repeat 5-10 times.

For cysts & tumors: Ginger compress can help to loosen stagnation, but do not apply on tumors for more than 5 minutes. Always follow immediately with taro plaster to draw out toxins.

NOTE: For some cancer conditions, ginger can be too stimulating. Consult a macrobiotic teacher, and the Cancer Prevention Diet, by Michio Kushi, for more information, before using for any cancer.

Relieves aches & pains

Stimulates lymphatic flow

Loosens & helps dissolve toxic accumulations (follow with taro plaster for cysts & tumors)

Ginger Sesame Spine Rub

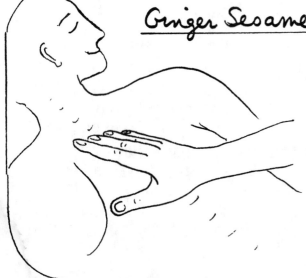

To help heal chronic back tension
Spinal curvatures
Nervous system disorders

Finely grate about 2 T. ginger. Squeeze this over a cup, to yield 1 tsp. ginger juice. Mix with 1 tsp. sesame oil. Massage into the muscles on both sides of the spine. Rub vigorously until the skin gets warm and red. Repeat daily.

HEALING FOOD	DESCRIPTION & USE	TRADITIONAL BENEFITS

KANTEN

(also called
  agar agar gel)

White flakes derived from a sea vegetable, used to make gelatins.

To relieve constipation from overly contractive diet: Dissolve 3 T. kanten or agar agar flakes in a mixture of 1½ c. apple juice & ½ c. water. Bring to a boil, then simmer 5 minutes. Add 1/4 tsp. grated ginger juice. Pour into a shallow dish to gel.

Helps relieve constipation from overly contractive diet

KUKICHA TWIG TEA

(also called

  Bancha Twig

  or just Twig)

Dark brown, roasted stems from the green tea plant. Taste is mild, yet substantial and satisfying. Contains traces of caffein (green bancha tea is much higher).

For a good daily beverage: Roast the whole package of twigs--to revive flavor-- by stirring in a skillet over medium heat for a few minutes. Store in a tightly sealed jar. Boil water and add about 1 tsp. per cup. Simmer 10 minutes or until desired strength. Re-use twigs 2 or 3 times...just add a little more water and fresh twigs.

For oncoming cold symptoms: Mix 1/2 - 1 tsp. tamari soy sauce with hot twig tea. Drink once or twice a day for up to 3 days.

Relieves fatigue

Good antidote for sweets
  (a buffer, it neutralizes
  over-acid blood conditions)

Helps combat oncoming cold
  and flu symptoms by
  alkalinizing the blood
  (for more alkaline effect,
  add a little tamari).

HEALING FOOD	DESCRIPTION & USE	TRADITIONAL BENEFITS

KUZU

Note: kuzu measurements are for a heaping spoonful

White root-starch (no flavor), made from 7 ft. long roots of the wild kuzu plant. Dissolves in cold water, thickens in hot. Use in daily cooking to thicken sauces, stews, puddings, Chinese vegetable combinations.

For vitalizing tea: Dissolve 1 heaping tsp. kuzu in 1 c. cool water. Add ½ tsp. mashed umeboshi plum, a few drops tamari soy sauce, and a pinch grated ginger (optional). Heat and stir until thick. Drink once a day.

Very alkalinizing & soothing

Renews strength & vitality

Controls diarrhea (tea)

Relieves upset stomach (tea)

Beneficial for colds, flu, or prolongued weakness (tea)

LOTUS ROOT TEA

Amber, powdered tea, made from water lily roots. Dissolve 2 tsp. in 1 c. water. Boil, then simmer 15 minutes. For stronger effect, buy fresh lotus root at an Oriental market. Grate and squeeze juice from ½ c. lotus. Add 1 c. water, boil, then simmer 15 minutes. Drink hot.

Soothes coughs

Helps dissolve mucus in lungs

MISO

Brown or amber fermented flavoring paste made from soy or other beans, grains, and sea salt. Buy unpasteurized (for live enzymes to aid digestion). Add to soups, stew, sauces, or dressings.

For healing soup: Use 2 year old barley, rice, or hatcho miso. Sweet & mellow varieties-- aged a shorter time--are less beneficial for healing (see p. 25).

Renews intestinal flora

Alkalanizes the blood

Helps cleanse nicotine and radioactive substances from the body

---

HEALING FOOD	DESCRIPTION & USE	TRADITIONAL BENEFITS
<u>RICE CREAM</u>	Soothing cereal made from pureed brown rice. Wash rice, then roast in a dry skillet, stirring until uniformly golden brown. Add 3 to 6 parts water, a pinch of sea salt, and pressure cook for 2 hours. Squeeze through a clean cheesecloth to extract a fine cream. Serve with a small amount of condiment such as tekka, sesame salt, umeboshi plum, or shiso. Eat as much as desired.	For debilitating illness when digestion is impaired
<u>TAMARI SOY SAUCE</u> (also called Shoyu) 	Naturally produced soy sauce made from soybeans, wheat, and sea salt. Original, wheat-free tamari was made by pouring off the juice from making hatcho miso--look for this if you have wheat allergies. <u>In daily cooking:</u> Use sparingly in soups, stir-fries, casseroles, dressings. Aim for a sweet taste--not heavily salted. <u>In tea:</u> To help relieve fatigue or oncoming colds, (see Kukicha Twig Tea).	Provides digestive enzymes Alkalanizes the blood
<u>TEKKA</u>	Crumbly, rich dark brown seasoning with savory flavor. Made from miso, burdock, carrot, lotus, ginger & salt. High in iron. Use sparingly, 1/2 tsp. daily to garnish meals.	Alkalanizes & cleanses blood Strengthens intestines Renews energy

HEALING FOOD	DESCRIPTION & USE	TRADITIONAL BENEFITS
TARO PLASTER	A gelatinous mixture made from brown-skinned, white fleshed taro potatoes, ginger, and flour. Used regularly as an external plaster, in combination with a self-healing diet, may help to reduce size of cysts and tumors by drawing toxins out through the skin (apply ginger compress first). NOTE--For breast cancer: ginger and taro can some-times be too stimulating. Consult with a macrobiotic counselor and your own intuition, before using. To make plaster: Buy small taro potatoes in Oriental grocery. Peel and grate enough to make 1/2" layer covering area. For each 1/2 c. taro, add 1 T. unbleached flour and 2 tsp. grated ginger. Spread on a clean cheesecloth and apply directly to the skin (after warming area with ginger compress). Change every 4 hours, or leave on overnight.	Draws toxins out through the skin Can help loosen toxic accumulations, and reduce cysts and tumors (for cancer, consult macrobiotic counselor, and see Cancer Prevention Diet, Michio Kushi).
TOFU PLASTER	A cooling compress made from fresh tofu (soybean curd), pastry flour, and ginger. Squeeze water from tofu and mash. Mix 6 parts tofu, 3 parts flour, and 1 part ginger. Spread on a cheesecloth and apply to forehead. Change every 2 hours, or sooner, if it gets hot.	To reduce fever
TWIG TEA	(see Kukicha Twig Tea, p. 199)	

HEALING FOOD	DESCRIPTION & USE	TRADITIONAL BENEFITS
UMEBOSHI PLUM	Pink-red, salt-pickled plums with pleasing sour, salty taste. Anti-bacterial action benefits intestines. Flavor stimulates appetite. Delicious cooked with sauteed vegetables, in dressings, or on fresh corn. However, these are easy to overdo in daily cooking... so tasty, but salty! 1-2 plums a week in plenty. For intestinal upsets, hangover, or fatigue: Add 1/2 tsp. mashed plum to a cup of twig tea.	Very alkalanizing Relieves temporary intestinal upsets Counteracts upset stomach, hangover, fatigue Helps detoxify the liver *Take these along when you travel.... good for "the runs"* 
UME EXTRACT	Thick, concentrated syrup made from umeboshi--all the alkalinizing benefits, without the salt. Very tangy, lemony flavor. For a quick pep-up, to relieve upset stomach, or help detox the liver: Dissolve a pea-size lump of ume extract in hot twig tea or hot water. Drink once daily, as needed.	As above

Green Heals

Many Oriental remedies are salty. For balance, it's important to remember that they are intended to accompany a daily diet high in fresh, chlorophyll-rich dark leafy greens-- especially if you live in a warm climate.

Humble greens....tops of radishes & turnips
Noble greens....kale, collards, mustards
Sprightly greens....watercress, parsley, bok choy

When you think healing, think green!

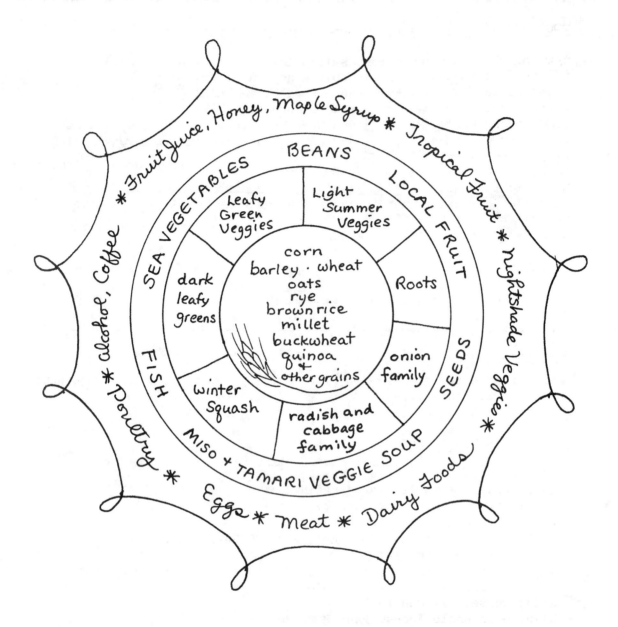

A centered diet is built around cooked whole grains
and seasonal vegetables as daily staples....
May we all enjoy the circumference in healthy measure.

Resources

COOKBOOKS (Dairy-free, low-fat, low-sweet)

Book of Whole Meals, Annemarie Colbin
Calendar Cookbook, Cornelia Aihara
Complete Guide to Macrobiotic Cooking, Aveline Kushi
Cooking for Regeneration, Cecil Tovah Levin
Feeding the Whole Family, Cynthia Lair
Fresh From a Vegetarian Kitchen, Meredith McCarty
Fruit-Sweet & Sugar-Free, Janice Feuer
Lenore's Natural Cuisine, Lenore Baum
Macro Mellow, Shirley Gallinger & Sherry Rogers, M.D.
Macrobiotic Cooking for Everyone, Edward & Wendy Esko
Natural Food Cookbook, Mary Estella
Sweet and Natural, Meredith McCarty

GARDENING

The Findhorn Garden, Findhorn Community
How To Grow More Vegetables, John Jeavons
The One Straw Revolution, Masanobu Fukuoka

Seed Catalogs:

Abundant Life Seed Foundation, P.O. Box 772, Port Townsend, WA 98363
Johnny's Selected Seeds, Albion, ME 04910
Territorial Seed Co., P.O. Box 27, Lorane, OR 94751

HEALING RESOURCE BOOKS

12 Stages of Healing, Donald Epstein, D.C.
Cancer Prevention Diet, Michio Kushi
The Cure Is In the Kitchen, Sherry Rogers, M.D.
Diet for a New America, John Robbins
Diet for a Small Planet, Rev. Ed., Frances Moore Lappe
Diet & Nutrition, Rudolph Ballentine, M.D.
Dr. Dean Ornish's Program for Reversing Heart Disease, Dean Ornish, M.D.
Food and Healing, Annemarie Colbin
Healing Ourselves, Naburo Muramoto
Healing With Whole Foods, Paul Pitchford
How to See Your Health: Book of Oriental Diagnosis, Michio Kushi
Love, Medicine and Miracles, Bernie Siegal, M.D.
Macrobiotic Family Health Care, Patrick McCarty & Shizuko Yamomoto
Macrobiotic Way, Michio Kushi
McDougall's Medicine, John McDougall, M.D.
Menopausal Years the Wise Woman Way, Susan Weed
Natural Healing, Michio Kushi
Natural Medicine for Children, Julian Scott, Ph.D., L.Ac.
Pre-Menstrual Syndrome Self-Help Book, Susan Lark, M.D.
Pritikin Promise: 28 Days to Longer Healthier Life, Nathan Pritikin
Recalled by Life, Anthony Satillaro
Serving Fire: Rhythms and Rituals of the Hearth, Anne Scott

HEALING RESOURCE BOOKS (continued)

Staying Healthy With Nutrition, Eldon Haas
Sugar Blues, William Dufty
The Way of Herbs, Michael Tierra
Wise Woman Herbal for the Childbearing Year, Susan Weed

CONTACTS FOR SELF-HEALING EDUCATION

Findhorn Foundation	International guest program demonstrating how to live in cooperation with spirit and nature. Write Findhorn, The Park, Forres, IV 36 OTZ, Scotland. Website: www.findhorn.org
Healing From the Body Level Up	3-5 day workshops in rapid ways to clear self-limiting patterns that can interfere with mind/body healing. Ph: (781) 453-0737. Website: www.jaswack.com
International BodyTalk Association	Trains health professionals and lay people in a pioneering health care system that creates optimal communication between brain and body. Write 5500 Bee Ridge Rd., Ste 103, Sarasota FL 34233. Website: www.bodytalksystem.com
Kushi Institute	Live-in macrobiotic study center, summer camps and weekend programs. Referrals to local teachers and cooks. Worldwide macrobiotic directory. Write P.O. Box 390, Becket, MA 01223. Ph: (800) 975-8744. Website: www.macrobiotics.org
Natural Gourmet Cookery School	Offers everything from quick, healthy meals to natural gourmet chef training. Write: 48 West 21st St., 2nd Fl., New York, NY 10010. Ph: (212) 645-5170.

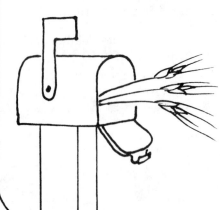

Recipe Index

KRISTINA TURNER first found joy in the kitchen
while inventing vegetarian feasts for 200 at the
Findhorn Community in Scotland.

Her pioneering and playful approach to macrobiotics
and healing has made this book a well-loved favorite
of cooking teachers and health professionals in
many countries around the world.

Kristina lives on Vashon Island, Washington, where
she enjoys being a mother, counselor, and a lifelong
student of what it takes to create vibrant community.

She extends a special thanks to you--
for becoming part of the growing wave of organic
farmers and natural food cooks who are nurturing
life for the generations to come.

To contact her, e-mail: kristinaturner@earthlink.net

 Printed on Recycled Paper